1001
EASY
GERMAN
PHRASES

M. Charlotte Wolf, Ph.D.

D0041411

DOVER PUBLICATIONS, INC., Mineola, New York

Bibliographical Note

1001 Easy German Phrases is a new work, first published by
Dover Publications, Inc., in 2011.

Library of Congress Cataloging-in-Publication Data

Wolf, M. Charlotte.
    1001 easy German phrases / M. Charlotte Wolf.
        p. cm. — (Dover language guides)
    Includes index.
    ISBN-13: 978-0-486-47630-8
    ISBN-10: 0-486-47630-8
    1. German language—Conversation and phrase books—English. I. Title.

    PF3121.A19 2011
    438.3'421—dc22

                                                        2011010623

Manufactured in the United States by LSC Communications
47630805   2019
www.doverpublications.com

Table of Contents

INTRODUCTION vii
    Hochdeutsch vs. Dialekt vii
    Pronunciation viii
    A Brief Guide to German Sounds viii
    Phonetic Transcription x
    Creating Phrases x

Chapter 1: Greetings and Everyday Expressions 1
    Greetings, Introductions, and Social Conversation 1
    Making Yourself Understood 8
    Useful Words and Expressions 10
    Describing Yourself and Others 15
    Difficulties and Repairs 17
    Numbers and Telling Time 20
    Talking About Times of Day, Days of the Week,
      and Months 23
    Talking About the Weather and Seasons 25

Chapter 2: Travel 28
    Travel: General Vocabulary and Expressions 28
    Tickets 30
    Traveling by Car 32
    Air Travel 34
    Customs and Baggage 36
    Traveling by Train 36
    Taking the Bus 38
    Taxi! 39
    Taking the Subway 41
    Traveling on Two Wheels 42
    Traveling on Foot 42
    At the Hotel 44

Chapter 3: Mealtimes 46
    Talking About Mealtimes and Eating: General Expressions 47

Dining Out   49
Menu: General Items   52
Breakfast Food   53
Appetizers, Lunch Items and Salad   55
Main Course   57
Fruits and Vegetables   58
Dessert   60
Beverages   62

Chapter 4: Socializing and Leisure   65
Houses of Worship   65
Friends and Social Networking   66
Sightseeing   67
Hobbies   70
Sports   72

Chapter 5: Shopping   73
Banking and Money   73
Shopping   74
Measurements   88
Colors   89

Chapter 6: Health   91
At the Pharmacy   91
At the Drugstore   93
Seeing a Doctor   95
Seeing a Dentist   98
Seeing an Optometrist   99

Chapter 7: Communications   100
Post Office   100
Telephone   101
Internet, Electronics, and Computers   103

**Chapter 8: Proverbs, Idiomatic Expressions, Cognates,
Interjections, Slang**   107
Proverbs   107
Idiomatic Expressions   111
Cognates   112
Interjections   113
Slang   114

**APPENDIX: LANGUAGE STRUCTURES AND PARTS
OF SPEECH** 117
    Nouns 117
        Articles and Gender 117
        Gender, Case, and Number 117
    Adjectives 119
    Adverbs 121
    Subject pronouns 122
    Verbs 122
        Conjugation 122
        Commands (Imperatives) 123
    Word Order 123
        Negation 124
        Extended Word Order 124
        Dependent Clauses 125

MORE LEARNING RESOURCES 127
INDEX 129

Introduction

1001 Easy German Phrases contains basic words and phrases that are useful for communication when traveling in Germany, Austria, and Switzerland, which is where German is most commonly spoken. In addition, German is still widely understood—and spoken—in eastern France (Lorraine and Alsaçe) and northern Italy ("Südtirol").

This book will also assist you with understanding German's structural qualities, such as grammar and syntax, as well as enabling you to express your needs and handle situations when traveling in any of the countries and regions mentioned above. While this book is tailored to your needs as a traveler, it is not intended as a comprehensive guide to the German language. However, since the material presented is not cumulative, you may pick and choose the chapter or section that is most useful to you in any given situation.

Hochdeutsch vs. Dialekt

People new to the German language may be in for a big surprise after arriving in Austria, Germany, or Switzerland for the first time, because the German they hear may not exactly match the German they *expected* to hear. Although standard German, or Hochdeutsch [HOCH-doytsh], is taught in schools and used in business, social, and tourist-related situations, there always comes a time when you suddenly experience "Bahnhof" [BAWN-houf]—the sensation of words coming at you like the noise at a train station! You have come face to face with one of the many dozens of dialects of German.

Hochdeutsch is the result of efforts to synchronize the many different regional variants that have existed since the early Middle Ages in the German-speaking parts of Europe. Faced with the multitude of different German dialects that obstructed communication among inhabitants from different German-speaking regions, people realized the need to come up with a standardized version that would be understood by all. So, thanks to Hochdeutsch, newspapers, books, and other publications from Hamburg to Vienna all display the same language, despite minor regional variations. The regional dialects have not ceased to exist, however, and when residents of the Austrian state of Tyrol, for example, speak among themselves, they are not using Hochdeutsch, but their regional dialect. Similarly, if you visit a local pub in a small coastal town in Northern Germany, you will hear people speak in "Plattdeutsch," or you will hear "Bairisch" spoken in the southern and southeastern parts of Germany, including the city of Munich. And anyone who has spent more than a day in German Switzerland knows that the spoken language, "Schwyzerdütsch" [SHVY-tseh-dootsh], is quite different from the Hochdeutsch used in Swiss newspapers or heard on Swiss TV and radio stations.

Pronunciation

Note that the phonetic transcription provided for each word and phrase is modeled closely after the sound and pronunciation patterns of English. In the tables that follow, you will find a description of German sounds that differ from English sounds. Together with the information provided in the section "Phonetic Transcription," this information will help you with the pronunciation of German words, phrases, and sentences.

A Brief Guide to German Sounds

Below you will find a brief description of German sounds that are markedly different from English. Sounds that are similar to ones found in English are not listed.

Vowels, including umlauts and diphthongs	sounds like	examples/English translation	phonetic transcription
A	"a" in "ah"	Ratte/rat	[RAH-te]
E	"e" in "yesterday"	Messer/knife	[MESS-ah]
I	always like "i" in "minister"	Minute/minute	[min-OO-teh]
O	"o" in "lost"	Vorhang/curtain	[FORE-hahng]

U	"oo" in "moose"	Musik/music	[moo-ZEEK]
ö	almost like "ew" in "new"	Öl/oil	[OEL]
ä	always like "a" in "man"	Lämmer/lambs	[LAEMM-ah]
ü	similar to "ew" in "new"	Nüsse/nuts	[NOU-sseh]
au	"ow" in "how"	blau/blue	[BLAU]
äu	"oy" in "boy"	Mäuse/mice	[MOY-zeh]
ei	"i" in "nice"	Preis/price	[PREIS]
eu	"oy" in "boy"	teuer/expensive	[TOY-ah]

Consonants	sounds like	examples/English translation	phonetic transcription
c	"ts"	Cäsar/Cesar	[TSAY-zah]
ch	"kh" (after a, o, u)	Rache/revenge	[RA-khe]
ch	"sh"(after i, ei, äu, eu, e)	Ich/I	[ISCH]
ck	"k"	Rock/skirt	[ROK]
g	"g"	Gier/greed	[GEER]
j	"y"	Ja/yes	[YAH]
v	"f" or "v"	viel/much; Vase/vase	[FEEL][VAH-ze]
w	"v"	Wasser/water	[VAS-eh]
y	"ew"	Zylinder/cylinder	[tsew-LIN-dah]
z	"ts"	Zar/czar	[TSAR]
ss, ß	"s"	Ross/horse	[ROHSS]

Phonetic Transcription

The numbered entries below are arranged in a consistent manner that includes the English phrase, its German translation, and a phonetic transcription. The phonetic transcription is intended to help you get a feel for how the German words and phrases you see printed here will sound, and is based on sounds that you are familiar with from the English language. Transcriptions appear in **boldface,** and are broken down into syllables separated by dashes; words are separated by spaces. Syllables in uppercase letters are stressed, while those in lowercase letters are not stressed (e.g., minister [MIN-is-tah]).

My name is Melanie.	(English phrase)
Ich heiße Melanie.	(German translation)
ISCH HEI-suh MEL-ah-nee	(phonetic transcription)

Try to get a feel for how to pronounce the phrase by practicing it.

Creating Phrases

You will also find it easy to form additional phrases and sentences using the ones provided. In instances where this is possible, simply use one of the alternatives listed below the example sentence.

I come from the U.S.	(English phrase)
Ich komme aus _____.	(German translation)
ISCH KOMM-e AUS	(phonetic transcription)

_____ den USA.
DAIN OO-ESS-AAH

_____ England.
ENG lant

_____ der Schweiz.
DEHR SHVEITZ

In the **Appendix,** you will find more useful information on how to form sentences in German.

Unlike English, German has formal and informal registers of address. These are indicated in the choice of the subject pronoun and the form of the verb. "Sie" is both the plural and singular second-person formal, while "ihr" and "du" are the informal plural and the informal singular second-person forms, respectively. Use the formal form of address for people whom you do not know well or who are older than you, and reserve the informal one for family, friends, and, in general, people under the age of sixteen. While Americans prefer to be informal in many situations, Germans prefer to interact formally. In the phrases throughout this book, you will find examples of both formal and informal forms of address. Take a look at the examples below.

Can you tell me where the nearest travel agency is?

When talking to one or more strangers, you would say:

Können Sie mir bitte sagen, wo das **nächste** Reisebüro ist?
  (formal singular or plural)
KOEN-en ZEE meer BIT-te ZA-gen VOH das NAYKH-steh
  REI-ze-bew-ro ist?

When talking to a group of two or more people you know, or to a group of children or adolescents, you would say:

Könnt ihr mir bitte sagen, wo das **nächste** Reisebüro ist?
  (informal plural)
KOENNT-EER meer BIT-teh ZA-gen VOH das NAYKH-steh
  REI-ze-bew-ro ist?

When talking to only one of your friends or family members, or a child or adolescent, you might say:

Kannst du mir bitte sagen, wo das **nächste** Reisebüroist?
  (informal singular)
KANNST doo meer BIT-the ZA-gen VOH das NAYKH-steh
  REI-ze-bew-ro ist?

To show politeness, greet a shopkeeper or hotel employee with "Guten Tag" instead of "Hallo" or "Tag." The final two expressions should be used with family and friends.

Unlike in the United States, people in Germany prefer to refer to themselves in a more impersonal way. This is particularly true when making general statements about a group of people—unless a German is speaking specifically about a group that includes her or him.

Thus, while you expect to hear Germans use the subject pronoun "wir" (which corresponds to the English "we"), you will hear them frequently use the pronoun "man" instead.

In Germany, we like to drink beer. (English)

*In Deutschland trinkt **man** gern Bier. (German)*

in-DOITSH-lant TRINKT mann GEHRN BEEYA

The gender of a noun usually has nothing to do with its biological status as female or male. While an adult male is indicated with "der" and an adult female with "die," such easy correspondences end there. A German girl, for example, is "das Mädchen," taking the neuter article. Although there are some rules for classifying nouns into one of the three genders (e.g., nouns ending in *–ling* are always masculine; nouns ending in *–ion* are always feminine; and nouns ending in *–lein* are always neuter), gender assignment generally is arbitrary, and it is imperative to memorize the article along with the noun. Finally, when referring to groups of mixed gender, German uses the plural article "die" in the nominative and accusative cases.

German nouns have masculine and feminine forms when they refer to nationality, profession, character, or appearance. For example, *der Amerikaner* refers to an American man; *die Amerikanerin* refers to an American woman. Other examples include *der Ingenieur/die Ingenieurin* (the engineer), *der Schöne/die Schöne* (the beauty), *der Zauberer/die Zauberin* (the magician). In such cases in this book, you will find listed both the masculine and feminine forms of the noun. When describing yourself, use the appropriate form of the noun, either masculine or feminine. Germans, when giving their nationality or profession, drop the article from the noun. For example, „ich bin Deutsche" (I am German; female); „ich bin Deutscher" (I am German; male). Or, „ich bin Lehrerin" (I am a teacher; female); „ich bin Lehrer" (I am a teacher; male). The dropping of the article occurs in second- and third-person forms, as well.

Chapter 1
Greetings and Everyday Expressions

GREETINGS, INTRODUCTIONS, AND SOCIAL CONVERSATION

1. Good morning. *Guten Morgen.* **GOO-ten MOR-gen**

2. Good evening. *Guten Abend.* **GOO-ten AH-bent**

3. Good night. (bedtime) *Gute Nacht.* **GOO-te NAHKT**

4. Hello. *Guten Tag (formal), Hallo (informal)*
   GOO-ten TAK [HAL oh]

5. Hi. *Tag.* **TAK**

6. Good-bye. *Auf Wiedersehen (formal), Tschüss (informal)*
   AUF VEE-da-zayn [CHOOS]

7. See you soon! *Bis bald!* **Biss BALLT**

8. See you later! *Bis später!* **Biss SHPAY-tah**

9. See you tomorrow! *Bis morgen!* **BISS MOR-gen**

10. Have a nice day! *Schönen Tag noch!*
    SHOEN-nen TAK nokh

11. My name is _____. *Ich heiße _____.* **isch HI-sseh**

12. Allow me to introduce you to _____. *(most formal)*
    Darf ich Ihnen _____ vorstellen?
    DAHRF isch EE-nen _____ FOR-shtell-en

My colleague. *(m.)*   *Mein Kollege.*   mine kol-EH-ge

My colleague. *(f.)*   *Meine Kollegin.*   **MY-ne** kohll-EH-ghin

Boyfriend. *(m.)*   *Mein Freund.*   mine **FROYNT**

Girlfriend. *(f.)*   *Meine Freundin.*   **MY–ne** FROYN-din

13.   This is _____.   *Das ist _____.*   **DASS** ist

    My wife.   *Meine Frau.*   **MY-ne** FROW

    My husband.   *Mein Mann.*   **MINE MAHN**

    My spouse/partner. *(m.)*   *Mein Lebensgefährte.*
    MINE LAY-bens-ge-FAIR-te

    My spouse/partner. *(f.)*   *Meine Lebensgefährtin.*
    MY-ne LAY-bens-ge-FAIR-tin

    My friend. *(m.)*   *Mein Freund.*   mine **FROINT**

    My friend. *(f.)*   *Meine Freundin.*   **MY-ne** FROIN-din

14.   My daughter.   *Meine Tochter.*   **MY-ne** TOKH-ta

    My son.   *Mein Sohn.*   mine **ZOHN**

    My child.   *Mein Kind.*   mine **KINT**

    My children.   *Meine Kinder.*   **MY-ne** KIN-da

    My brother.   *Mein Bruder.*   **MINE BREW-da**

    My sister.   *Meine Schwester.*   **MY-ne** SHVES-ta

    My family.   *Meine Familie.*   **MY-ne** fam-EE-lee-ah

15.   Pleased to meet you.   *(Sehr) Angenehm.*
    (ZEHR) AN-ge-name

16.   How nice to see you again. *(formal, singular and plural)*
    Wie schön, Sie wiederzusehen!
    vee SHOEN zee VEE-da-tsoo-zayn

    Nice to see you again. *(informal, singular)*
    Schön, dich wiederzusehen!
    SHOEN disch VEE-da-tsoo-zayn

17.   I am here on a business trip.   *Ich bin geschäftlich hier.*
    isch bin ge-SHEFT-lish HE-ah

18.   We're on vacation.   *Wir machen Ferien.*
    VEE-ah makh-en FAY-ree-en.

19. I work for _____.   *Ich arbeite für _____.*
    isch AHR-bi-te FEWAH _____.

20. What line of work are you in?
    Was machen Sie beruflich? (formal)
    vas MAKH-en-zee ba-ROOF-lish

    Was machst du beruflich? (informal)
    vas MAKHST doo ba-ROOF-lish

21. Where do you work?   *Wo arbeiten Sie? (formal)*
    voh AHR-bite-en zee

22. *Wo arbeitest du? (informal)*   voh AHR-bite-est doo

23. I am _____.   *Ich bin _____.*   isch BIN

    _____ a stay-at-home mom.
    _____ *Hausfrau und Mutter.*
    HOWS-frow unt MOOT-e

    _____ a doctor.   _____ *Arzt. (m.) Ärztin. (f.)*
    AHRTST   EHRS-tin

    _____ a teacher.   _____ *Lehrer. (m.) Lehrerin. (f.)*
    LAIR-ah   LAIR-a-rin

    _____ a university professor.
    _____ *Universitätsprofessor. (m.) Universitätsprofessorin. (f.)*
    ooni-ver-see-TAITS-pro-FESS-ah
    ooni-ver-see-TAITS-pro-fess-OR-in

    _____ a businessman.
    _____ *Kaufmann. (m.) Kauffrau. (f.)*
    KOWF-mann   KOWF-frow

    _____ an architect.   _____ *Architekt. (m.) Architektin. (f.)*
    AR-kee-TEKT   AR-kee-TEKT-in

    _____ an engineer.
    _____ *Ingenieur. (m.) Ingenieurin. (f.)*
    ON-zhe-NOOR   ON-zhe-NOOR-in

    _____ a scientist.
    _____ *Wissenschaftler. (m.) Wissenschaftlerin. (f.)*
    VISS-en-shahft-ler   VISS-en-shahft-ler-in

24. I am retired.   *Ich bin Rentner. (m.)*   isch bin RENT-na
    Ich bin Rentnerin. (f.)   isch bin RENT-na-rin

25. I am currently unemployed.   *Ich bin zur Zeit arbeitslos.*
    isch bin tsooah TSEIT AHR-bites-los

26. I'm a college student.   *Ich bin Student. (m.)/ Studentin. (f.)*
    shtoo-DENT   shtoo-DENT-in

27. I'm studying_____.   *Ich studiere_____.*
    isch shtoo-DEE-re

    | _____ | English. | _____ | *Englisch.* | ENG-lish |
    | _____ | History. | _____ | *Geschichte.* | ge-SHISH-te |
    | _____ | German. | _____ | *Deutsch.* | DOITSH |
    | _____ | Biology. | _____ | *Biologie.* | bee-oh-low-GEE |
    | _____ | Chemistry. | _____ | *Chemie.* | khe-MEE |

    _____ Engineering.
    _____ *Ingenieurwissenschaften.*
    ON-zhe-NOOR-viss-en-SHAFT-ten

28. I am a friend of Robert's.
    Ich bin ein Freund von Robert. (if you are male)
    isch bin ein FROIND fon RO-beaht

    Ich bin eine Freundin von Robert. (if you are female)
    isch bin eye-ne FROIN-din fon RO-beaht

29. How are you?   *Wie geht es Ihnen? (formal)*
    vee GAIT ess EE-nen

    Wie geht's? (informal)   vee GAITS

30. Fine, thanks. And you?   *Gut, danke. Und Ihnen? (formal)*
    GOOT DAHN-ke oont EE-nen

    Gut, danke. Und dir? (informal)
    GOOT DAHN-ke oont DEE-ah

31. All right.   *Es geht so.*   es GAIT zow

32. Very well.   *Sehr gut.*   ZAIR goot

33. Where are you from?
    Woher kommen Sie? (formal, singular or plural)
    VOH-HARE KOMM-en ZEE

    Woher kommt ihr? (informal, plural)
    VOH-HARE KOMMT EEAH

Woher kommst du? (informal, singular)
VOH-HARE KOMMST doo

I am from Boston.   *Ich komme aus Boston.*
isch KOMM-eh AUS BOS-tn

34. I am American.   *Ich bin Amerikaner. (m.)*
isch bin ah-mer-ee-KAH-nah

Ich bin Amerikanerin. (f.)   **isch bin ah-mer-ee-KAH-ne-rin**

35. Are you German?   *Sind Sie Deutscher? (m.) (formal)*
ZINT zee DOITSH-er

Sind Sie Deutsche? (f.) (formal)   **ZINT zee DOITSH-e**

Bist du Deutscher? (m.) (informal)   **BIST doo DOITSH-er**

Bist du Deutsche? (f.) (informal)   **BIST doo DOITSH-e**

36. How is your family?   *Wie geht es Ihrer Familie? (formal)*
VEE GAIT ess EE-rah fam-EE-lee-ah

Wie geht es deiner Familie? (informal)
VEE GAIT ess DINE-ah fam-EE-lee-ah

37. How are your friends?   *Wie geht es Ihren Freunden? (formal)*
VEE GAIT ess EE-ren FROIN-den

Wie geht es euren Freunden? (informal, plural)
VEE GAIT ess OI-ren FROIN-den

Wie geht es deinen Freunden? (informal, singular)
VEE GAIT ess DINE-en FROIN-den

38. Please have a seat.   *Bitte setzen Sie sich. (formal)*
BITT-eh ZETS-en ZEE SISCH

Bitte setzt Euch. (informal, plural)   **BITT-eh ZETST OISH**

Bitte setz dich. (informal, singular)   **BITT-eh ZETS DISCH**

39. What a pleasure to meet you. *(formal)*
Wie schön, Sie kennenzulernen!
VEE SHOEN zee KENN-en-tsoo-LAIR-nen

Nice to meet you. *(informal)*   *Schön, dich kennenzulernen.*
SHOEN disch KENN-en-tsoo-LAIR-nen

40. What a pleasant dinner.   *Was für ein angenehmes Abendessen.*
VAS fewah ein AN-ge-NAME-es AH-bent-ESS-en

41.   Give my regards to your family.
      Grüssen Sie Ihre Familie von mir. (formal, singular)
      GREW-sen zee EE-reh fam-EE-lee-eh fon MEE-ah

      Grüss deine Familie von mir. (informal, singular)
      GREWS DYNE-eh fam-EE-lee-eh fon MEE-ah

42.   Come visit us.
      Besuchen Sie uns doch. (formal, singular or plural)
      be-ZOOKH-en zee oons DOKH

      Besucht uns doch. (informal, plural)
      be-ZOOKHT oons DOKH

      Besuch uns doch. (informal, singular)
      be-ZOOKH oons DOKH

43.   Come back and see us.
      Besuchen Sie uns doch wieder. (formal, singular or plural)
      be-ZOOKH-en ZEE oons dokh VEE-da

      Besucht uns doch wieder. (informal, plural)
      be-ZOOKHT oons dokh VEE-da

      Besuch uns doch wieder. (informal, singular)
      be-ZOOKH oons dokh VEE-da

44.   We would love to visit you.
      Wir würden Sie gern besuchen. (formal, singular or plural)
      VEE-uh VUE-den zee gehrn be-ZOOKH-en

      Wir würden Euch gern besuchen. (informal, plural)
      VEE-uh VUE-den OISH gehrn be-ZOOKH-en

      Wir würden dich gern besuchen. (informal, singular)
      VEE-uh VUE-den disch gehrn be-ZOOKH-en

45.   Can I visit you sometime?
      Darf ich Sie besuchen? (formal, singular or plural)
      DAHF isch ZEE be-ZOOKH-en

      Darf ich euch besuchen? (informal, plural)
      DAHF isch OISH be-ZOOKH-en

      Darf ich dich besuchen? (informal, singular)
      DAHF isch disch be-ZOOKH-en

May I stop over and see you?
Darf ich bei Ihnen vorbeischauen? (formal, singular or plural)
DAHF isch bye EE-nen for-BYE-show-n

Darf ich bei euch vorbeischauen? (informal, plural)
DAHF isch bye OISH for-BYE-show-n

Darf ich bei dir vorbeischauen? (informal, singular)
DAHF isch bye DEE-ah for-BYE-show-n

46. What is your address?
Wie lautet Ihre Adresse? (formal, singular or plural)
VEE LAU-tet EE-re a-DRESS-e

Wie lautet eure Adresse? (informal, plural)
VEE LAU-tet OI-re a-DRESS-e

Wie lautet deine Adresse? (informal, singular)
VEE LAU-tet DINE-e a-DRESS-e

47. What is your phone number?
Wie lautet Ihre Telefonnumer? (formal, plural or singular)
VEE LAU-tet EE-re tell-e-FOHN-noom-uh

Wie lautet eure Telefonnumer? (informal, plural)
VEE LAU-tet OI-re tell-e-FOHN-noom-uh

Wie lautet deine Telefonnummer? (informal, singular)
VEE LAU-tet DYE-ne tell-e-FOHN-noom-uh

48. What is your email address?
Wie lautet Ihre Email-Adresse? (formal, singular or plural)
VEE LAU-tet EE-re EE-male ah-DRESS-e

Wie lauten eure Email-Adressen? (informal, when addressing a group)
VEE LAU-ten OI-re EE-male ah-DRESS-en

Wie lautet deine Email-Adresse? (informal, singular)
VEE LAU-tet DIE-ne EE-male ah-DRESS-e

49. Here is my address.   *Hier ist meine Adresse.*
HEE-ah ist mine-e ah-DRESS-e

50. Here is my cellphone number.   *Hier ist meine Handynummer.*
HEE-ah ist mine-e HAN-dee-NEW-mah

51. Here is my web site address.
Hier ist meine Webseitenadresse.
HEE-ah ist mine-e VEB-zei-ten-ah-DRESS-e

MAKING YOURSELF UNDERSTOOD

When approaching a stranger to ask a question, remember to show politeness by starting with "Entschuldigen Sie, bitte" [ent-SHOOL-dig-en-zee-BIT-te] when addressing an unfamiliar person or a supervisor, or saying "Entschuldige, bitte" [ent-SHOOL-dig-e-BIT-te] when addressing a friend or a person younger than sixteen.

52.   Do you speak English?
Sprechen Sie englisch? (formal, singular or plural)
SHPREKH-en zee ENG-lish

Sprecht ihr englisch? (informal, plural)
SHPREKHT EE-ah ENG-lish

Sprichst du englisch? (informal, singular)
SPRIKHST doo ENG-lish

53.   Does anyone here speak English?
Spricht hier jemand Englisch?
SPRIKHT HEE-ah YAY-mund ENG-lish

54.   I speak a little German.   *Ich spreche ein bisschen deutsch.*
isch SPREKH-e EIN BIS-schen DOITSH

55.   I only speak English.   *Ich spreche nur englisch.*
isch SPREKH-e NOOR ENG-lish

56.   I don't speak German well.
Ich spreche nicht sehr gut deutsch.
isch SPREKH-e NISCHT zair goot DOITSH

57.   Can you translate this word?
Können Sie dieses Wort übersetzen? (formal, singular or plural)
KOEN-en zee DEE-zes VORT oe-beh-ZETS-en

Könnt ihr dieses Wort übersetzen? (informal, plural)
KOENNT EE-ah DEE-zes VORT oe-buh-ZETS-en

Kannst du dieses Wort übersetzen? (informal, singular)
KAHNNST doo DEE-zes VORT oe-buh-ZETS-en

58.   What is the English equivalent of this phrase?
Wie lautet die englische Übersetzung für _____?
VEE LAU-tet dee ENG-lish-e oe-buh-ZETS-oong fewr

59. I understand.   *Verstanden.*   **fe-SHTAND-en**

60. I don't understand.   *Ich verstehe (das) nicht.*
    isch fa-SHTAY-eh (dass) NISHT

61. Do you understand?   *Haben Sie (das) verstanden?*
    HA-ben zee (dass) fe-SHTAN-den

62. Do you understand me?
    Können Sie mich verstehen? (formal, singular or plural)
    KOENN-en zee MISH fe-SHTAY-en

    Könnt ihr mich verstehen? (informal, plural)
    KOENNT EE-ah mish fe-SHTAY-en

    Kannst du mich verstehen? (informal, singular)
    KANNST DOO mish fe-SHTAY-en

63. Say it again, please.
    Bitte wiederholen Sie das! (formal, singular or plural)
    BIT-e vee-duh-HOLE-en ZEE DASS

    Bitte wiederholt das! (informal, plural)
    BIT-e vee-duh-HOLT DASS

    Bitte wiederhol das! (informal, singular)
    BIT-e vee-duh-HOLE DASS

64. Please speak more slowly, please.
    Bitte sprechen Sie langsamer! (formal, singular or plural)
    BIT-e SHPRE-khen zee LANG-zam-ah

    Bitte sprecht langsamer! (informal, plural)
    BIT-e SHPREKHT LANG-zam-ah

    Bitte sprich langsamer! (informal, singular)
    BIT-e SHPRISH LANG-zam-ah

65. Write it down, please.
    Können Sie das bitte niederschreiben? (formal, singular or plural)
    KOENN-en zee dass BIT-e NEE-da-shry-ben

    Könnt ihr das bitte niederschreiben? (plural)
    KOENNT EE-a dass BIT-e NEE-da-shry-ben

    Kannst du das bitte niederschreiben? (informal, singular)
    KANNST DOO dass BIT-e NEE-da-shry-ben

66. What does this mean?   *Was heißt das?*   **VASS HEIST dass**

67. How do you say "dog" in German?
    Wie sagt man "dog" auf deutsch?
    VEE zagt mann DAWG auf-DOITSH

68. What does this mean in English?
    Was heißt das auf Englisch?
    VASS HEIST dass auf ENG-lish

USEFUL WORDS AND EXPRESSIONS

69. Yes.   *Ja.*   **YA**

70. No.   *Nein.*   **NINE**

71. Maybe.   *Vielleicht.*   **fe-LYESHT**

72. Please.   *Bitte (sehr).*   **BIT-e zair**

73. Thanks (a lot).   *Danke (schön).*   **DAHN-ke shoen**

74. Thanks, that's very kind!   *Danke, das ist sehr nett!*
    DAHN-ke dass ist ZAIR net

75. You're welcome.   *Bitte.*   **BIT-e**

76. Pardon?   *Wie bitte?*   **VEE BIT-e**

77. Please excuse me.   *Entschuldigen Sie, bitte.*
    ent-SHOOL-dig-en zee BIT-e

78. (I am) sorry! (apology)   *(Das) tut mir leid!*
    DASS toot-MEE-a LITE

79. Fantastic!   *Fantastisch!*   **fan-TAST-ish**

80. Unbelievable!   *Unglaublich!*   **UN-GLAUB-lish**

81. Excellent!   *Ausgezeichnet!*   **AUS-ge-TSEISH-net**

82. Marvelous!   *Fabelhaft!*   **FAH-bell-haft**

83. Wonderful!   *Wunderbar!*   **VOON-dah-bah**

84. Can I help you?
Kann ich Ihnen helfen? (formal, singular or plural)
KANN isch EE-nen HEL-fen

Kann ich euch helfen? (informal, plural)
KANN isch OISH HEL-fen

Kann ich dir helfen? (informal, singular)
KANN isch DEE-ah HEL-fen

85. Please come in.   *Bitte treten Sie ein. (formal)*
BIT-e TRAY-ten zee EIN

Bitte tretet ein. (informal, plural)   **BIT-e TRAY-tet EIN**

Bitte tritt ein. (informal, singular)   **BIT-e TRIT EIN**

86. Come here.
Kommen Sie bitte her. (formal, singular or plural)
KOM-en zee BIT-e HEE-ah

Kommt bitte her. (informal, plural)   **KOMT BIT-e HAY- a**

Komm bitte her. (informal, singular)   **KOM-BIT-e-HAY- a**

87. I am in a hurry.   *Ich bin in Eile.*   **ISCH bin in EYE-le**

88. I am late.   *Ich bin spät dran.*   **ISCH bin SHPAIT DRAN**

89. I am hungry.   *Ich habe Hunger.*   **ISCH HA-be HOONG-a**

90. I am thirsty.   *Ich habe Durst.*   **ISCH HA-be DOORST**

91. I am tired.   *Ich bin müde.*   **ISCH bin MEW-da**

92. I am sorry.   *Es tut mir leid.*   **ES toot MEE-a LITE**

93. What's wrong?   *Was ist los?*   **VASS ist LOWSS**

94. Is something the matter?   *Was ist los?*
VASS ist LOWSS

95. It's ok.   *Es ist (schon) in Ordnung.*
ESS ist SCHON in ORD-noong

96. I know.   *Ich weiss.*   **ISCH VISE**

97. I don't know.   *Ich weiss es nicht.*   **ISCH VISE ess NISHT**

98. That's all.   *Das ist alles.*   **DASS ist ALL-es**

99. It doesn't matter.   *Schon gut.*   **SHON goot**

100. It's not serious.   *Es ist nichts Ernstes.*
ESS ist NISHTS ERNST-ess

101. Can you help me?
Können Sie mir helfen? (formal, singular or plural)
KOEN-en zee MEE-a HELF-en

Könnt ihr mir helfen? (informal, plural)
KOENNT EE-a MEE-a HELF-en

Kannst du mir helfen? (informal, singular)
KANNST doo MEE-a HELF-en?

102. Can you tell me?
Können Sie mir bitte sagen . . . ? (formal, singular or plural)
KOENN-en zee MEE-a BIT-e ZA-gen

Könnt ihr mir bitte sagen . . . ? (informal, plural)
KOENNT EE-a MEE-a BIT-e ZA-gen

Kannst du mir bitte sagen . . . ? (informal)
KANNST doo MEE-a BIT-e ZA-gen

103. Where is the restroom?   *Wo ist die Toilette?*
VOH ist dee toy-LET-e

104. Leave me alone!   *Lass mich in Ruhe!*
LASS MISH in ROO-e

105. I am looking for _____.   *Ich suche _____.*
isch ZOO-khe

_____ my hotel.   _____ *mein Hotel.*
   MINE ho-TELL

_____ the train station.   _____ *den Bahnhof.*
   dain BAHN-hof

_____ a restaurant.   _____ *ein Restaurant.*
   EIN ress-tau-RANT

_____ a bank.   _____ *eine Bank.*   **EYE-ne BAHNK**

106. Who?   *Wer?*   **VER**

107. What?   *Was?*   **VASS**

108. Why? *Warum?* **va-RUMM?**

109. Where? *Wo?* **VOH**

110. When? *Wann?* **VANN**

111. How much? *Wieviel?* **vee-FEEL**

112. How long/much time? *Wie lange?* **vee LANG-e**

113. What for? *Wofür?* **voh-FEWR**

114. To. *Zu, nach.* **TSOO NAKH**

115. From. *Von.* **FON**

116. With. *Mit.* **MIT**

117. Without. *Ohne.* **OH-ne**

118. In. *In.* **IN**

119. On. *Auf.* **OWF**

120. Near. *Bei.* **BYE**

121. Far. *Weit.* **VITE**

122. In front of. *Vor.* **FOR**

123. Behind. *Hinter.* **HINT-e**

124. Next to. *Neben.* **NAY-ben**

125. Outside. *Draussen, aussen.* **DROW-sen OW-sen**

126. Inside. *Drinnen, innen.* **DRINN-en INN-en**

127. Empty. *Leer.* **LAIR**

128. Full. *Voll.* **FOLL**

129. Something. *Etwas.* **ET-vass**

130. Nothing. *Nichts.* **NISHTS**

131. Several. *Einige.* **EYE-nig-e**

132. (Much) more. *(Viel) mehr.* **(FEEL) mare**

133. Less. *Weniger.* **VAY-nig-ah**

134. (A little) more. *(Ein bisschen) mehr.*
(EIN BISS-schen) mare

135. Enough. *Genug.* **ge-NOOG**

136. Too much. *Zu viel.* **tsoo FEEL**

137. Many. *Viel, viele.* **FEEL, FEEL-e**

138. Very. *Sehr.* **ZAIR**

139. Good. *Gut.* **GOOT**

140. Bad. *Schlecht.* **SHLESCHT**

141. Now. *Jetzt.* **YETST**

142. Later. *Später.* **SHPAYT-ah**

143. Immediately. *Sofort.* **zow-FORT**

144. Soon. *Bald.* **BALT**

145. As soon as possible. *Sobald wie möglich.*
zow-BALT vee MOEG-lish

146. It is (too) late. *Es ist (zu) spät.* **ESESS ist TSOO SHPAYT**

147. It is (too) early. *Es ist (zu) früh.* **ESS IST TSOO frew**

148. Slowly. *Langsam.* **LANG-zam**

149. Slower. *Langsamer.* **LANG-zam-ah**

150. Quickly. *Schnell.* **SHNELL**

151. Quicker. *Schneller.* **SHNELL-ah**

152. Look out! *Passen Sie auf! (formal, singular or plural)*
PASS-en zee AUF
Passt auf! (informal, plural) **PASST AUF**
Pass auf! (informal, singular) **PASS AUF**

153.   Listen!   *Hören Sie zu! (formal, singular or plural)*
       HOE-ren zee TSOO
       Hört zu! (informal, plurals)   **HOERT TSOO**
       Hör zu! (informal, singualr)   **HOER TSOO**

154.   Look!   *Schauen Sie her! (formal, singular or plural)*
       SHAU-en zee HAY-a
       Schaut her! (informal, plural)   **SHAUT HAY-a**
       Schau her! (informal, singular)   **SHAU HAY-a**

DESCRIBING YOURSELF AND OTHERS

155.   What does he/she look like?   *Wie sieht er/sie aus?*
       vee ZEET air aus vee ZEET zee aus

156.   Can you describe her/him?
       Können Sie sie/ihn beschreiben? (formal, singular or plural)
       KOENN-en ZEE zee be-SHRY-ben   KOENN-en zee EEN be-SHRY-ben
       Könnt ihr sie/ihn beschreiben? (informal, plural)
       KOENNT EER ZEE be-SHRY-ben   KOENNT EER EEN be-SHRY-ben
       Kannst du sie/ihn beschreiben? (informal)
       KANNST DOO zee be-SHRY-ben KANNST DOO EEN be-SHRY-ben

157.   He is young/old.   *Er/sie ist jung/alt.*
       AY-a ist (zair) YOONG/ALT   ZEE ist (zair) YOONG/ALT

158.   He has _____ eyes.   *Er hat _____e Augen.*
       AY-a hat_____ AU-gen
       blue.   *blau.*   **BLAU**
       green.   *grün.*   **GRUEN**
       brown.   *braun.*   **BROWN**
       hazel.   *haselnussbraun.*   **HA-zell-nouss-brown**
       gray   *grau.*   **GRAU**

159.   She has _____ hair.   *Sie hat _____e Haare.*
       ZEE hat _____ Ha-re

She has _____ eyes. *Sie hat _____ e Augen.*
ZEE hat _____ AU-gen

black. *schwarz.* **SHWARTS**

blond. *blond.* **BLOND**

red. *rot.* **ROHT**

160. He has _____ hair. *Er hat _____ -e Haare.*
AY-a hat_____ -e-HA-re

short. *kurz.* **KOURTS**

long. *lang.* **LANG**

straight. *glatt.* **GLATT**

curly. *lockig.* **LOK-isch**

161. She's a _____. *Sie ist _____.* **ZEE ist**

redhead. *rothaarig.* **ROHT-HAH-risch**

brunette. *brünett.* **brew-NET**

162. He's bald. *Er hat eine Glatze.* **AY-a hat EYE-ne GLAT-tseh**

163. She has _____. *Sie hat _____.* **ZEE HAT**

freckles. *Sommersprossen.* **SOMM-e-SHPROSS-en**

164. He has a beard and a mustache.
Er hat einen Vollbart und einen Schnauzer.
AY-a hat EYE-nen FOLL-bart oont EYE-nen SHNOW-tseh

165. I have _____. *Ich habe _____.* **isch HA-be**

a tattoo. *eine Tätowierung.* **EYE-ne tae-tow-VEE-roong**

some piercings. *piercings.* **PEE-a-sings**

166. She/he is very tan. *Sie/er ist sehr braungebrannt.*
ZEE/AY-a ist zair BROWN-ga-brannt

167. He/she is so beautiful. *Er/sie ist so schön.*
AY-a /ZEE ist zoh SHOEN

168. She/she is ugly. *Sie/er ist hässlich.* **ZEE/ AY-a ist HAESS-lish**

169. He/she is of medium build. *Er/sie ist mittelgroß.*
AY-a /ZEE ist MITT-ell-grohs

170. I am _____. *Ich bin _____.* **isch BIN**

_____ tall.   _____ *groß*.   **GROHS**

_____ short.   _____ *klein*.   **kline**

_____ (very) thin.   _____ *(sehr) schlank*.
(ZAIR) SHLANK

_____ (not very) fat.   _____ *(nicht sehr) dick*.
(NISCHT zair)-DIK

171. I weigh 70 kilos.   *Ich wiege 70 Kilo.*
ISCH VEE-ge ZEEB-tsish KEE-loh

172. I'm 1.75 meters tall.   *Ich bin 1,75 m groß.*
ISCH bin EYE-nen-MAY-te-FUENF-oont-ZEEB-tsish GROHS

173. What a(n.) _____ child!   *Was für ein _____-es Kind!*
VAS fewr ein _____ ess KINT

adorable!   *bezaubernd!*   **be-TSOW-bernt**

cute.   *süß!*   **ZEWS**

174. She/he is quite _____.   *Sie/er ist ganz _____.*
Zee/ay-a ist gants

_____ serious.   _____ *ernst*.   **AYNST**

_____ funny.   _____ *lustig*.   **LOOS-tisch**

_____ intelligent.   _____ *intelligent*.   **in-tell-ee-GENT**

175. He / she isn't _____.   *Er/sie ist nicht _____.*
AY-a/ZEE ist NISCHT

mean.   *böse*.   **BEW-ze**

rude.   *unhöflich*.   **OON-hoef-lisch**

176. She/he seems _____.   *Sie/er wirkt _____.*   **Zee/er virkt**

_____ calm.   _____ *ruhig*.   **ROO-isch**

_____ happy.   _____ *glücklich*.   **GLEWK-lisch**

_____ depressed.   _____ *deprimiert*.   **de-prim-EE-aht**

DIFFICULTIES AND REPAIRS

177. I cannot find my hotel address.
Ich kann die Adresse meines Hotels nicht finden.
ISCH kann dee a-DRESS-e MINE-ess ho-TELS nischt FIN-den

178. Can you help me?   *Können Sie mir helfen? (formal)*
      KOENN-en ZEE meer HEL-fen

      Könnt ihr mir helfen? (informal, when addressing a group)
      KOENNT EE-a MEE-a HEL-fen

      Kannst du mir helfen? (informal, singular)
      KANNST doo MEE-a HEL-fen

179. Help! (in the case of an emergency)   *Hilfe!*   **HILL-fe**

180. I have lost _____.   *Ich habe _____ verloren.*
      ISCH HA-be _____ fa-LAW-ren

      _____ my keys.   _____ *meine Schlüssel.*
          MY-ne SHLEWSS-ell

      _____ my passport.   _____ *meinen Reisepass.*
          MY-nen RISE-ay-pahss

181. Right now I'm looking for _____.
      Ich suche gerade nach _____.
      ISCH ZOO-khe ge-RA-de

      _____ my wallet.   _____ *meinem Geldbeutel.*
          MY-nem GELT-boi-tell

      _____ my purse.   _____ *meiner Handtasche.*
          MY-nah HANN-tash-e

      _____ my ticket.   _____ *meiner Fahrkarte.*
          MY-nah FAHR-kar-te

182. Have you seen _____?
      Haben Sie _____ gesehen? (formal)
      HA-ben ZEE_____ ge-ZAY-en

      Habt ihr _____ gesehen? (informal, when addressing groups)
      HABT EE-ah _____ ge-ZAY-en

      Hast du _____ gesehen? (informal, singular)
      HAST doo _____ ge-ZAY-an

      _____ my husband.   _____ *meinen Mann_____?*
          MY-nen MANN?

      _____ my wife?   _____ *meine Frau _____?*
          MY-ne FRAU

      _____ my (boy)friend?   _____ *meinen Freund _____?*
          MY-nen FROYND

_____ my (girl)friend?

_____ *meine Freundin* _____?

MY-ne FROYN-din

183. I forgot _____.   *Ich habe* _____ *vergessen.*
ISCH HA-be _____ **fa-GUESS-en**

_____ my money.   _____ *mein Geld*_____.
MINE GELT

_____ my traveler's checks.

_____ *meine Travelerschecks* _____.
MY-ne TRAV-el-ah-shecks

_____ my ATM card.

_____ *meine Scheckkarte* _____.
MY-ne SHEK-kar-te

_____ my credit card.

_____ *meine Kreditkarte* _____.
MY-ne kred-IT-kar-te

184. I have missed _____.   *Ich habe* _____*verpasst.*
ISCH HA-be_____**fa-PASST**

_____ my bus.   _____ *meinen Bus* _____.
MY-nen BOUSS

_____ my train.   _____ *meinen Zug* _____.
MY-nen TSOOK

_____ my plane.   _____ *meinen Flug* _____.
MY-nen FLOOK

185. What should I do?   *Was soll ich (bloß) tun?*
VAS ZOLL isch blohs TOON

186. Can you help me contact _____.
Können Sie mir helfen, _____ *zu kontaktieren? (formal, singular or plural)*
KOENN-en zee ME-ya HEL-fen _____ **TSOO kon-tak-TEE-ren**

Könnt ihr mir helfen, _____ *zu kontaktieren? (informal, plural)*
KOENNT EE-a ME-ya HEL-fen _____ **TSOO kon-tak-TEE-ren**

Kannst du mir helfen, _____ zu kontaktieren? (informal, singular)
KANNST DOO ME-ya HEL-fen _____ TSOO kon-tak-TEE-ren

_____ my family?   _____ *meine Familie* _____?
MY-ne fah-MEE-lee-e

_____ my colleague?
_____ *meinen Kollegen (m.)* _____?
_____ *meine Kollegin (f.)* _____?
        MY-nen koll-EH-gen   MY-ne koll-EH-gin

187. My glasses are broken.   *Meine Brille ist kaputt.*
     MY-ne BRILL-e ist ka-PUT

188. Where can I get them repaired?
     Wo kann ich sie reparieren lassen?
     VOH kann isch zee re-par-EE-ren LASS-en

189. I need a new hearing aid.   *Ich brauche ein Hörgerät.*
     isch BROW-khe ein HOER-ge-rait

190. This is my medication.   *Das sind meine Medikamente.*
     DASS ZINT MY-ne me-di-ka-MEN-te

191. Where is the lost-and-found desk?   *Wo ist das Fundbüro?*
     VOH ist dass FOONT-bew-roh

192. Is the American consulate nearby?
     Ist das amerikanische Konsultat in der Nähe?
     ist dass AH-mair-e-KAHN-e-she kon-soo-LAT in de NAY-e

193. I'm looking for the police station.
     Ich suche das Polizeirevier.
     isch ZOO-khe dass poh-lee-TSEYE-re-VEE-ah

194. I am going to call a policeman.   *Ich rufe die Polizei.*
     isch ROO fe dee poh-lee-TSEYE

NUMBERS AND TELLING TIME

In Germany and other German-speaking countries, the 24-hour-clock system is used for transportation schedules as well as other official situations (for example, radio, television, and newspapers). Seven o'clock in the morning would be given as "7 Uhr morgens" [ZEE-ben OO-ah MOR-gens], whereas seven o'clock at night would be "19 Uhr" [NOIN-tsehn OO-ah]. An easy way to convert the 24-hour clock to the American clock is to subtract 12 from the hours of the afternoon and evening.

When telling time informally, Germans use "Viertel nach" [FEER-tl NAKH], "Viertel vor" [FEER-tl FAW-a], and "halb" [HALP] to indicate times other than the full hour. "Viertel nach" means "a quarter past" and "viertel vor" means "a quarter to" the hour. "Halb" indicates that one is "half way" to the next hour. So, "viertel nach drei" means "a quarter after three," while "halb vier" means three-thirty, and "viertel vor vier" means "a quarter to four."

When talking informally, Germans often drop "Minuten" and "Uhr" when giving the time. Thus, "zehn Minuten nach sieben Uhr" can be shortened to "zehn nach sieben."

195. One. *Eins.* **EYNTS**

196. Two. *Zwei.* **TSVYE**

197. Three. *Drei.* **DRY**

198. Four. *Vier.* **FEE-a**

199. Five. *Fünf.* **FEUNF**

200. Six. *Sechs.* **ZEKHS**

201. Seven. *Sieben.* **ZEE-bn**

202. Eight. *Acht.* **AKHT**

203. Nine. *Neun.* **NOIN**

204. Ten. *Zehn.* **TSAYN**

205. Eleven. *Elf.* **ELF**

206. Twelve. *Zwölf.* **TSVOELF**

207. Thirteen. *Dreizehn.* **DRY-tsehn**

208. Fourteen. *Vierzehn.* **FEE-a-tsehn**

209. Fifteen. *Fünfzehn.* **FOENF-tsehn**

210. Sixteen. *Sechzehn.* **ZEKH-tsehn**

211. Seventeen. *Siebzehn.* **ZEEB-tsehn**

212. Eighteen. *Achtzehn.* **AKHT-sehn**

213. Nineteen. *Neunzehn.* **NOIN-tsehn**

214. Twenty. *Zwanzig.* **TSVAN-tsisch**

215. Twenty-one. *Eiunundzwanzig.* **EIN-oont-tsvan-tsisch**

216. Twenty-two. *Zweiundzwanzig.* **TSVEYE-oont-tsvan-tsisch**

217. Twenty-three. *Dreiundzwanzig.* **DRY-oont-tsvan-tsisch**

218. Twenty-four. *Vierundzwanzig.* **FEE-a-oont-tsvan-tsisch**

219. Twenty-five. *Fünfundzwanzig.* **FEUNF-oont-tsvan-tsisch**

220. What time is it? *Wie spät ist es? Wieviel Uhr ist es?*
VEE SHPAIT ist ess VEE-feel OO-ah ist ess

221. It is seven o'clock. *Es ist sieben. (Uhr)*
ESS ist ZEE-bn OO-ah

222. It is nine o'clock in the morning. *Es ist neun Uhr morgens.*
ESS ist NOIN OO-ah MOR-gens

223. Is it three-thirty? *Ist es halb vier?* **IST ess HALP FEE-ah?**

224. No, it's three forty-five. *Nein, es ist Viertel vor vier.*
NINE ess ist FEER-tl FOH-ah FEE-ah

225. It is morning. *Es ist Morgen.* **ESS ist MOR-gen**

226. It's noon. *Es ist Mittag.* **ESS ist MIT-ak**

227. It is afternoon. *Es ist Nachmittag.*
ESS ist NAKH-mit-tak

228. It's midnight. *Es ist Mitternacht.* **ESS ist MIT-a-nakht**

229. My train arrives at a quarter to ten.
      Mein Zug kommt um Viertel vor zehn an.
      MINE-TSOOK komt oom FEER-tal FOH-ah TSEHN unn

230. At ten minutes past seven.   *Um zehn (Minuten) nach sieben.*
      OOM TSEHN (mee-NOO-tan) nukh SEE-ban

TALKING ABOUT TIME OF DAY, DAYS OF THE WEEK , AND MONTHS

231. Today.   *Heute.*   **HOY-te**

232. Tomorrow.   *Morgen.*   **MOR-gen**

233. Yesterday.   *Gestern.*   **GUESS-tern**

234. Day after tomorrow.   *Übermorgen.*   **UE-be-mor-gen**

235. Week.   *Die Woche.*   **dee VAW-khe**

236. See you tomorrow!   *Bis morgen!*   **biss MOR-gen**

237. Next week.   *Nächste Woche.*   **NAYKH-ste VAW-khe**

238. See you next week!   *Bis nächste Woche!*
      biss NAYKH-ste VAW-khe

239. Last week.   *Letzte Woche.*   **LETS-te VAW-khe**

240. Day.   *Der Tag.*   **dair TAK**

241. Month.   *Der Monat.*   **dair MOW-not**

242. Year.   *Das Jahr.*   **dass YAH**

243. Next year.   *Nächstes Jahr.*   **NAYKH-stes YAH**

244. See you next year!   *Bis nächstes Jahr!*
      biss NAYKH-stes YAH

245. Last year.   *Letztes Jahr.*   **LETS-tes YAH**

246. We met each other last year.
      Wir haben uns letztes Jahr getroffen.
      VEE-ah HA-ben oons LETS-tes YAH ge-TROFF-en

247. I work on _____.   *Ich arbeite am* _____.
     isch AR-bey-te am

     Mondays.   *Montag.*   **MOWN-tak**

     Tuesdays.   *Dienstag.*   **DEENS-tak**

     Wednesdays.   *Mittwoch.*   **MIT-vawkh**

     Thursdays.   *Donnerstag.*   **DON-es-tak**

     Fridays.   *Freitag.*   **FRY-tak**

     Saturday.   *Samstag, Sonnabend.*   **ZAMS-tak, ZAWN-ah-bent**

     Sunday.   *Sonntag.*   **SAWN-tak**

248. I have a meeting this Saturday.
     Ich habe am Samstag einen Termin.
     isch HA-be ahm ZAMS-tak EYE-nen ter-MEEN

249. What day is it today?   *Was für ein Tag ist heute?*
     VASS fewr ein TAK ist HOI-te

250. Today is Friday.   *Heute ist Freitag.*   **HOI-te ist FRY-tak**

251. I'll be in Paris next _____.
     Ich bin in Paris nächst- _____.
     isch bin in pa-REES NAYKHST _____

     _____ *-e Woche.*   **e VAW-khe**

     _____ *.-es Jahr.*   **es YAH**

     _____ *.-en Montag.*   **en MOWN-tak**

252. January.   *Der Januar.*   **dair YAHN-oo-ah**

     February.   *Der Februar.*   **dair FAYB-roo-ah**

     March.   *Der März.*   **dair MAERTS**

     April.   *Der April.*   **dair ah-PRILL**

     May.   *Der Mai.*   **dair MEYE**

     June.   *Der Juni.*   **dair YOON-ee**

     July.   *Der Juli.*   **dair YOOL-ee**

     August.   *Der August.*   **dair au-GOOST**

     September.   *Der September.*   **dair zep-TEM-ba**

     October.   *Der Oktober.*   **dair ok-TOH-ba**

November.   *Der November.*   dair no-VEM-ba

December.   *Der Dezember.*   dair de-TSEM-ba

253. Our appointment is for March 4th.
      Unser Termin ist am 4. März.
      OON-za ter-MEEN ist ahm FEE-ah-ten MAERTS

254. Next month.   *Nächsten Monat.*   **NAIKHS-ten MOH-naht**

255. Last month.   *Letzten Monat.*   **LETS-ten MOH-naht**

256. When is your birthday? *(formal, singular or plural)*
      Wann haben Sie Geburtstag?
      VANN HA-bn zee ge-BOORTS-tak?

      When is your birthday? *(informal, plural)*
      Wann habt ihr Geburtstag?
      VANN habt EE-ah ge-BOORTS-tak?

      When is your birthday? *(informal, singular)*
      Wann hast du Geburtstag?
      VANN hast doo ge-BOORTS-tak?

257. My birthday is April 16th.
      Mein Geburtstag ist am 16. April.
      MINE ge-BOORTS-tak ist ahm-ZEKH-tsayn-ten ah-PRILL

TALKING ABOUT THE WEATHER AND SEASONS

258. What's the weather like today?   *Wie ist das Wetter heute?*
      VEE ist dass VET-ah HOY-te

259. What's the forecast for tomorrow?
      Wie wird das Wetter morgen?
      VEE VEE-aht dass VET-ah MOR-gen

260. I love/dislike the climate here.
      Ich liebe/hasse das Klima hier.
      isch-LEE-be dass KLEE-ma HEE-ah isch HASS-e dass KLEE-ma HEE- ah

261. Back home it's _____.   *Bei uns zuhause ist es _____.*
      bye OONS tsoo-HOW-ze ist ess

_____ sunnier.   _____ *sonniger.*   **ZAWNN-igg-a**

_____ more humid.   _____ *schwüler.*   **SHVEW-lah**

_____ hotter.   _____ *heißer.*   **HI-sah**

262. It's sunny.   *Es ist sonnig.*   **ESS ist zawnn-isch**

263. It's cloudy.   *Es ist wolkig.*   **ESS ist VOLL-kisch**

264. It's windy.   *Es ist windig.*   **ESS ist VIN-disch**

265. It's cold.   *Es ist kalt.*   **ESS ist KAHLT**

266. It's hot.   *Es ist heiß.*   **ESS ist HEISS**

267. What a heatwave!   *Was für eine Hitze!*
     VASS FEWR EYE-ne HITS-e

268. It's (very) chilly.   *Es ist (sehr) kalt.*   **ESS ist (ZAIR) KAHLT**

269. It's snowing.   *Es schneit.*   **ESS SHNITE**

270. It's raining.   *Es regnet.*   **ESS RAYG-net**

271. The weather is dreadful!   *Das Wetter ist schrecklich.*
     dass VET-ah ist SHREK-lisch

272. What's your favorite season?
     Was ist Ihre liebste Jahreszeit? (formal, singular or plural)
     VASS ist EE-re LEEB-ste YAH-ress-tsite

     Was ist eure liebste Jahreszeit? (informal, plural)
     VASS ist OI-re LEEB-ste YAH-ress-tsite

     Was ist deine liebste Jahreszeit? (informal, singular)
     VASS ist DINE-e LEEB-ste YAH-ress-tsite

273. I prefer _____.   *Mir ist _____ lieber.*
     MEE-ah ist _____ LEE-be
     Winter.   *Der Winter.*   **dair WIN-tah**
     Spring.   *Der Frühling.*   **dair FREW-ling**
     Summer.   *Der Sommer.*   **dair ZOM-ah**
     Fall.   *Der Herbst.*   **dair HERBST**

274. I really dislike _____.   *Ich mag _____ überhaupt nicht!*
     ISCH mawg _____ EWE-be-HOWPT nicht

| _____ the heat. | _____ *Hitze*. | **HITS-e** |
| _____ the cold. | _____ *Kälte*. | **KELL-te** |

275. Next summer. *Nächsten Sommer.*
NAYKH-sten ZAWMM-ah

276. Last fall. *Letzten Herbst.* **LETS-ten HAIRBST**

Chapter 2
Travel

TRAVEL: GENERAL VOCABULARY AND EXPRESSIONS

277. Excuse me, where is _____?
      Entschuldigung, wo ist _____?
      ent-SHOOL-dee-goong VOH ist

      _____ downtown.   _____ *die Innenstadt.*
                 dee INN-en-shtat

      _____ the shopping district.
      _____ *das Einkaufsviertel.*
                 dass EIN-kowfs-FEER-tl

      _____ the residential neighborhood.
      _____ *das Wohnviertel.*
                 dass VOHN-feer-tl

278. Is this the right direction?   *Ist das die (richtige) Richtung?*
      IST dass dee (RISCH-tee-ge) RISCH-toong?

279. To the right?   *Nach rechts?*   **nakh REKHTS**
      To the left?   *Nach links?*   **nakh LINKS**

280. Is it on this side of the street?   *Ist es auf dieser Straßenseite?*
      IST ess auf DEE-zah SHTRASS-en-ZITE-e

281. Is it on the other side of the street?
      Ist es auf der anderen Straßenseite?
      IST ess auf dair-AN-deren SHTRASS-en-ZITE-e

282. At the corner?
      An der Ecke? An der Ecke (street name) und (street name)?
      AN dair ECK-e _____-oont-_____

283. Across the street?
Auf der anderen Straßenseite?
AUF dair AN-deren STRASS-en-ZITE-e

284. In the middle?   *In der Mitte?*   **IN dair MIT-e**

285. Straight ahead?   *Geradeaus?*   **ge-RAH-de-AUS**

286. Forward.   *Vorwärts.*   **FAW-ah-VAIRTS**

287. Back.   *Zurück.*   **tsoo-REWK**

288. In front of.   *Vor.*   **FAW-ah**

289. Behind.   *Hinter.*   **HIN-tah**

290. Next to.   *Neben.*   **NAY-bn**

291. To the right of.   *Rechts von.*   **REKHTS fawn**

292. To the left of.   *Links von.*   **LINKS fawn**

293. To the north.   *Nördlich von.*   **NOERD-lisch fawn**

294. To the south.   *Südlich von.*   **SEWD-lisch fawn**

295. To the east.   *Östlich von.*   **OEST-lisch fawn**

296. To the west.   *Westlich von.*   **VEST-lisch fawn**

297. What is the address?   *Wie ist die Adresse?*
VEE ist dee uh-DRESS-e

298. What street is this?   *Welche Straße ist das?*
VEL-she STRASS-e IST dass

299. Where is the nearest travel agency?
Wo ist das nächste Reisebüro?
VOH ist dass NAYKHS-te REIZE-e-BEWR-oh

300. Can you help me make a reservation?
Können Sie mir mit der Reservierung helfen?
KOENN-en zee meer MIT dair re-ze-VEE-roong HEL-fn

301. How long is the trip between _____ and _____?
Wie lange dauert die Reise von _____ nach _____?
**vee LANG-e DOW-ert dee REIZE-e fawn _____ nahkh
_____**

302.   Where can I get a (train) schedule?
       Wo kann ich einen Fahrplan bekommen?
       VOH kann isch EIN-en FAHR-pluhn be-KOMM-en

303.   Will I need my passport?   *Brauche ich meinen Reisepass?*
       BROW-khe isch MINE-en RISE-ay-pass

304.   Do I need a visa to visit this country?
       Brauche ich ein Visum für dieses Land?
       BROW-khe isch ein VEE-oom fewr DEE-zes LANT

305.   I missed _____.
       Ich habe _____ verpasst.
       isch HA-be _____ fah-PASST

       _____ my flight.   _____ *meinen Flug* _____.
          MINE-en FLOOK

       _____ my train.   _____ *meinen Zug* _____.
          MINE-en TSOOK

       _____ my local bus.   _____ *meinen Bus* _____.
          MINE-en BOOSS

       _____ my intercity bus.
       _____ *meinen Intercitybus* _____.
          MINE-en INT-e-SIT-ee-booss

       _____ my shuttle.   _____ *mein Shuttle* _____.
          MINE SHUT-tl

       _____ my ride.
       _____ *meine Mitfahrgelegenheit* _____.
          MINE-e MIT-FAHR-ge-LAY-gen-hite

TICKETS

306.   Ticket.   *der Fahrschein.*   **dair FAHR-shine**

307.   First class.   *Erste Klasse.*   **AIR-ste KLASS-e**

308.   Second class.   *Zweite Klasse.*   **TSWITE-e KLASS-e**

309.   A reserved seat.   *Ein reservierter Platz.*
       EIN re-ze-VEE-ah-tah PLATS

310.   Discounted-rate ticket.   *Ein Billigticket.*
       EIN BILL-isch-TICK-et

311. Group discount. *Ein Gruppenrabatt.*
      EIN GROOP-en-rah-BATT

312. Student discount. *Ein Studentenrabatt.*
      EIN shtoo-DENT-en-rah-BATT

313. Senior discount. *Ein Seniorenrabatt.*
      EIN zen-ee-awe-en-rah-BATT

314. I need to go to the Lufthansa ticket counter.
      Ich muss zum Lufthansa Ticketschalter gehen.
      **isch MOUSSE tsoom LOOFT-an-zah TICK-et-
      SHALT-e GAY-en**

315. How much does this ticket cost?
      Wieviel kostet dieses Ticket?
      VEE-feel KOST-et DEE-zes TICK-et

316. Where is the ticket window? *Wo ist der Schalter?*
      VOH ist dair SHALT-ah

317. I'd like to buy a one-way ticket.
      Ich möchte eine einfache Fahrkarte.
      isch MEWSH-te EIN-ne EIN-fakh-e FAHR-kar-te

318. I'd like to buy a round-trip ticket.
      Ich möchte eine Rückfahrkarte.
      isch MEWSH-te EIN-ne REWK-fahr-kar-te

319. I'd like a first-class ticket.
      Ich möchte eine Fahrkarte erster Klasse.
      isch MEWSH-te EIN-e FAHR-kar-te AIRS-te KLASS-e

320. Is this ticket refundable?
      Gibt es eine Rückerstattung für dieses Ticket?
      GIPT es ein-e REWK-air-SHTATT-oong fewr DEE-zes TICK-et

321. Is it possible to change dates?
      Kann ich die Reisedaten ändern?
      KANN isch dee REIZ-e-DA-ten EN-dairn

322. Is it possible to have another seat?
      Kann ich einen anderen Platz haben?
      KANN isch EIN-en AN-de-ren PLATS HA-bn

323. I would like a seat _____.
Ich möchte einen Platz _____.
isch MEWSH-te EIN-en PLATS

_____ next to my husband.
_____ neben meinem Mann.
NAY-bn MINE-em MANN

_____ next to my wife.   _____ neben meiner Frau.
NAY-bn MINE-ah FRAU

_____ next to the window.   _____ neben dem Fenster.
NAY-bn daym FENS-tah

_____ next to the aisle.   _____ am Gang.   am GANG

324. Can I book a reservation online?
Kann ich eine online Reservierung machen?
KANN isch EIN-e ON-line re-ze-VEER-oong MAKH-en

325. Is this an e-ticket?   Ist das ein elektronisches Ticket?
IST dass EIN e-lek-TRAWN-isch-es TICK-et

326. May I have a copy of my itinerary?
Kann ich eine Kopie meines Reiseplans haben?
KANN isch EEIN-e kaw-PEE MY-nes REIZ-e-plawns HA-bn

TRAVELING BY CAR

327. A car.   Ein Auto.   EIN AU-toh

328. A car rental agency.   Eine Autovermietung.
EIN-e AU-toh-fa-MEET-oong

329. I'd like to rent a car.   Ich möchte ein Auto mieten.
isch MEWSH-te EIN AU-toh-MEET-en

330. What are your rates?   Wie sind ihre Raten?
VEE sint EE-re RAH-ten

331. Do I need to pay a deposit?   Muss ich eine Kaution zahlen?
MOUSSE isch EIN-e KOW-tsee-OWN TSAH-len

332. A driver's license.   Ein Führerschein.   EIN FEWR-ah-shine

333. Do I need an international driver's license?
      Brauche ich einen internationalen Führerschein?
      BROW-khe isch EIN-en IN-te-nats-ee-own-AH-len FEWR-ah-shine

334. Comprehensive insurance.   *Vollkaskoversicherung.*
      FOHLL-kass-kaw-fe-ZISH-e-roong

335. Does this price include comprehensive insurance?
      Ist Vollkaskoversicherung im Preis eingeschlossen?
      ist FOHLL-kass-kaw-fe-ZISH-e-roong im PREIS EIN-ge-shloss-en

336. To drive.   *Fahren.*   **FAH-ren**

337. I am driving from Berlin to Hamburg.
      Ich fahre von Berlin nach Hamburg.
      isch fah-re fawn beah-LEEN nakh HAM-boork

338. Do you have a map of the area?
      Haben Sie eine Straßenkarte von dieser Gegend?
      HA-ben zee EIN-e SHTRASS-en-kahr-te fawn DEE-zer GAY-gent

339. Where is the nearest gas station?
      Wo ist die nächste Tankstelle?
      VOH ist dee NAYKH-ste TANK-shtel-e

340. I need to have my car fixed.
      Ich muss mein Auto reparieren lassen.
      isch MOUSSE mine AU-toh re-pah-REE-ren LASS-en

341. My car is broken down.   *Ich habe eine Autopanne.*
      isch HA-be EIN-e AU-toh-PAN-e

342. I can't start the car.   *Mein Auto springt nicht an.*
      mine AU-toh SHPRINGT nischt AN

343. The battery is dead.   *Die Batterie ist leer.*
      Dee batt-ah-REE ist LAIR

344. I am out of gas.   *Mein Benzintank ist leer.*
      mine ben-ZEEN-tank ist LAIR

345. I have a flat tire.   *Ich habe einen platten (Reifen).*
      isch HA-be EIN-en PLAT-en (RIFE-n)

346. The engine is overheating.   *Der Motor überhitzt.*
      dair moh-TOR ew-be-HITST

347. I think it needs water.
      Ich glaube, der Motor braucht Wasser.
      isch GLOW-be dair moh-TOR BROWKHT VASS-ah

348. There is a leak.   *Hier ist ein Leck.*   **HEE-ah ist ein LEK**

349. Is there a garage nearby?   *Gibt es hier eine Autowerkstatt?*
      GIPT ess HEE-ah EIN-e AU-toh-VAIRK-shtat

350. Can you tow me to the nearest garage?
      *Können Sie mein Auto zur nächsten Autowerkstatt
      abschleppen?*
      **KOENN-en ZEE mine AU-toh tsoor naykh-sten AU-toh-
      VAIRK-shtat AP-shlep-en**

AIR TRAVEL

351. Airport.   *Der Flughafen.*   **dair FLOOK-HA-fen**

352. How can I get to the airport?
      Wie komme ich zum Flughafen?
      VEE KOM-e isch tsoom FLOOK-HA-fen

353. Is this there a shuttle for the airport?
      Gibt es hier ein Shuttle zum Flughafen?
      GIPT ess HEE-ah ein SHUT-l tsoom FLOOK-ha-fen

354. Airline.   *Fluglinie.*   **FLOOK-li-nee-e**

355. I am flying on Lufthansa.   *Ich fliege Lufthansa.*
      isch FLEE-ge LOOFT-an-sah

356. Where do I check my bags?
      Wo kann ich mein Gepäck einchecken?
      VOH kann isch mine ge-PECK EIN-tsheck-en

357. I'd like to confirm my reservation on _____.
      Ich möchte meine Reservierung mit _____bestätigen.
      **isch MEWSH-te MY-ne re-ze-VEER-oong MIT _____ be-
      STAY-ti-gen**

358.   Do I need a boarding pass?   *Brauche ich eine Bordkarte?*
BROW-khe isch EIN-e BORT-ka-te

359.   My flight is leaving at 7:45 in the morning.
Mein Flug geht um Viertel vor acht.
MINE FLOOK gait oom FEER-tl fawr AKHT

360.   Is the flight late?   *Ist mein Flug spät dran?*
IST mine FLOOK shpait DRAN?

361.   When is the next flight to Vienna(Wien)?
Wann geht der nächste Flug nach Vienna (Wien)?
VANN gait dair NAYKHS-te FLOOK nakh VEEN

362.   Is this a direct flight?   *Ist das ein Direktflug?*
IST dass ein dee-REKT FLOOK

363.   How many bags may I check?
Wieviele Koffer darf ich einchecken?
VEE-FEEL-eah KOFF-ah DARF isch EIN-tsheck-en

364.   Where is the check-in for my flight?
Wo kann ich mein Gepäck einchecken?
VOH KANN isch mein ge-PECK EIN-tsheck-en

365.   Where is the departure gate?   *Wo ist der Flugsteig?*
VOH ist dair FLOOK-shteig

366.   Can I bring this on board?
Kann ich das mit an Bord nehmen?
KANN isch dass mit an BORT nay-men

367.   Where is the baggage claim?   *Wo ist die Gepäckausgabe?*
VOH ist dee ge-PECK-aus-GA-be

368.   Where is the luggage from the flight from _____?
Wo ist die Gepäckausgabe für den Flug aus _____?
VOH ist dee ge-PECK-aus-GA-be FEWR dain FLOOK aus

369.   We have jet lag.   *Wir haben Jet-Lag.*
VEE-ah HA-bn JET-lak

CUSTOMS AND BAGGAGE

370. Where is the customs?   *Wo ist die Zollabfertigung?*
VOH ist dee TSOLL-ahp-FAIR-tee-goong

371. Where is the passport check?   *Wo ist die Passkontrolle?*
VOH ist dee PAHSS-kon-trawll-e?

372. I'm here on a stop-over on my way to _____.
*Ich bin hier für einen Zwischenstopp auf dem Weg nach
_____.*
**isch bin HEE-ah fewr ein-en TSVISH-en-shtawp auf daym
VAYK nakh**

373. My passport.   *Mein Pass.*   **mine PAHSS**

374. Here are my bags.   *Hier ist mein Gepäck.*
HEE-ah ist mine ge-PECK

375. I have nothing to declare.   *Ich habe nichts zu verzollen.*
ISCH ha-be NISCHTS tsoo fe-TSAWLL-en

376. This is for my personal use.
Das ist für meinen persönlichen Gebrauch.
DASS ist fewr MINE-en pear-ZEWN-lisch-en ge-BROWKH

377. How much do I pay?   *Wieviel muss ich bezahlen?*
VEE-FEEL mousse isch be-TSAH-len

378. I'd like to leave these bags at the baggage office.
Ich möchte dieses Gepäck im Büro der Gepäckausgabe lassen.
**isch MEWSH-te dee-zes ge-PECK im bewr-EAU dair ge-
PECK-AUS-GAH-be LASS-en**

TRAVELING BY TRAIN

379. Train Station.   *Bahnhof.*   **BAHN-hohf**

380. Where is the train station?
Wo ist der Bahnhof?
VOH ist dair BAHN-hohf

381. When does the train for Frankfurt leave?
Wann fährt der Zug nach Frankfurt ab?
VANN fairt dair tsook nakh FRANK-foort AP

382. The platforms are over there.
Die Bahnsteige sind hier drüben.
dee BAHN-shteig-e ZINT hee-ah DREW-ben

383. Is this the right platform for the train to Linz?
Ist das der Bahnsteig für den Zug nach Linz?
ist DASS dair BAHN-shteig fewr dayn TSOOK nakh LINTS

384. Is this the train for Freiburg?
Ist das der Zug nach Freiburg?
ist DASS dair TSOOK nakh FRY-boork

385. Is this the train from Berlin?   *Ist das der Zug aus Berlin?*
ist DASS dair TSOOK aus bear-LEEN?

386. Does this train stop at Würzburg?
Hält dieser Zug in Würzburg?
HELLT DEE-zah TSOOK in VEWRTS-boork?

387. Stamp your ticket.
Entwerten Sie Ihren Fahrschein. (formal, singular or plural)
ent-VAIR-ten ZEE EE-ren FAHR-shine

Entwertet euren Fahrschein. (informal, plural)
ent-VAIR-tet OI-ren FAHR-shine

Entwerte deinen Fahrschein. (informal, singular)
ent-VAIR-te DIE-nen FAHR-shine

388. What time does the train from Leipzig arrive?
Wann kommt der Zug aus Leipzig an?
VANN kommt dair TSOOK AUS LEIP-tsisch AHN?

389. I'd like to buy a ticket on the Intercity train to Hamburg.
Ich möchte eine Fahrkarte für den Intercity nach Hamburg kaufen.
isch MEWSH-te ein-e FAWR-kar-te fewr dayn IN-te-SITT-ee nakh HAM-boork kauf-fen

390. Is there a connection?
Gibt es einen Anschluss nach _____?
GIPT ess EIN-en AN-shlooss nakh

391. How much time do I have to make the connection?
Wie lange ist der Zwischenstopp?
VEE lang-e ist dair TSVISH-en-shtop?

392. We have to make our connection.
Wir müssen unseren Anschluss erreichen.
VEE-ah MEWSS-en OON-ze-ren AHN-schlooss air-REISH-en

393. We have two reserved seats.
Wir haben zwei reservierte Plätze.
VEE-ah ha-ben TSVEYE re-ze-VEER-te PLAIT-tse

394. Tickets, please.   *Die Fahrkarten, bitte.*
dee FAWR-kar-ten BIT-e

395. This seat is taken.   *Dieser Platz ist besetzt.*
DEE-zah PLATS ist be-ZETST

396. Where is the dining car?   *Wo ist der Speisewagen?*
VOH ist dair SHPEIZ-e-VA-gen

397. I almost missed my train.
Ich habe beinahe meinen Zug verpasst.
ISCH ha-be BYE-nah-e mine-en TSOOK fa-PASST

398. Does this train have Wi-Fi?   *Gibt es Wifi in diesem Zug?*
GIPT ess VIE-FIE in DEE-zem TSOOK

TAKING THE BUS

399. Bus station.   *Der Busbahnhof.*   **dair BOOSS-bahn-hohf**

400. Intercity bus.   *Der Überlandbus.*   **dair EW-be-lant-booss**

401. I would like a schedule, please.
Ich möchte bitte einen Fahrplan.
isch MEWSH-te BIT-e ein-en FAHR-plan

402. Local bus.   *Der Lokalbus.*   **dair low-KALL-boos**

403. Bus stop.   *Die Bushaltestelle.*
dee BOOSS-HALL-te-shtell-e

404. A book of 10 tickets, please.
Ich möchte bitte einen Zehnerpass.
isch MEWSH-te BIT-e ein-en TSAY-ne-PASS

405. Is there a bus that goes to _____?
Gibt es hier einen Bus nach _____?
GIPT ess hee-ah ein-en BOOSS nakh

406. Which route do I have to take?
Welche Linie muss ich nehmen?
VEL-sche LEE-nee-e mousse isch NAY-men

407. Where do I get the bus to go to _____?
Wo finde ich den Bus nach _____?
voh FINN-de isch dain BOOSS nakh

408. What time is the first bus?   *Wann geht der erste Bus?*
VANN gayt dair ERS-te BOOSS

409. When does the last bus leave?   *Wann geht der letzte Bus?*
VANN gayt dair LETS-te BOOSS

410. Where is the nearest bus stop?
Wo ist die nächste Bushaltestelle?
VOH ist dee NAYKHS-te BOOSS-hall-te-shtell-e?

411. Does this bus stop downtown?
Hält dieser Bus in der Innenstadt?
HELLT dee-zah BOOSS in dair INN-en shtat?

412. Can you please tell me where to get off?
Wo muss ich aussteigen?
VOH mousse isch AUS-shteig-en

413. The next stop, please.   *Die nächste Haltestelle, bitte.*
dee naykhs-te HALL-te-shtell-e BIT-e

414. Will I need to change buses?   *Muss ich umsteigen?*
MOUSSE isch OOM-shteig-en?

TAXI!

415. Taxi stand.   *Der Taxistand.*   **dair TAK-see-shtant**

416. Where can I get a taxi?   *Wo gibt es hier ein Taxi?*
VOH gipt ess hee-ah ein TAK-see?

417. Can you please call a taxi?
Können Sie mir bitte ein Taxi rufen? (formal, singular or plural)
KOENN-en zee meer BIT-e ein TAK-see roof-en?

Könnt ihr mir bitte ein Taxi rufen? (informal, plural)
KOENNT EE-ah meer BIT-e ein TAK-see roof-en?

Kannst du mir bitte ein Taxi rufen? (informal, singular)
KANNST doo meer BIT-e ein TAK-see roof-en?

418. Would you like to share a taxi?
Möchten Sie ein Taxi mit mir teilen? (formal, singular or plural)
MEWSH-ten zee ein TAK-see mit meer TILE-en?

Möchtet ihr ein Taxi mit mir teilen? (informal, plural)
MEWSH-tet EE-ah ein TAK-see mit meer TILE-en?

Möchtest du ein Taxi mit mir teilen? (informal, singular)
MEWSH-test doo ein TAK-see mit meer TILE-en?

419. How much is the fare into town?
Wieviel kostet eine Fahrt in die Stadt?
vee-FEEL kost-et ein-e FAHRT in dee SHTAT

420. I'd like to go to _____.   *Ich möchte _____.*
isch MEWSH-te

_____ the airport.   _____ *zum Flughafen.*
tsoom FLOOK-hah-fen

_____ the train station.   _____ *zum Bahnhof.*
tsoom BAHN-hohf

_____ the bus station.   _____ *zur Bushaltestelle.*
tsoor BOOSS-hall-te-shtell-e

421. I'm in a hurry.   *Ich bin in Eile.*   **isch bin in EYE-le**

422. Is it far?   *Ist es weit?*   **IST ess VITE**

423. Here's the address.   *Hier ist die Adresse.*
HEE-ah ist dee a-DRESS-e

424. Can you stop here, please?
Können Sie hier bitte halten? (formal, singular or plural)
KOENN-en zee hee-ah BIT-e HALL-ten

Könnt ihr hier bitte halten? (informal, plural)
KOENNT EE-ah hee-ah BIT-e HALL-ten

Kannst du hier bitte halten? (informal, singular)
KANNST doo hee-ah BIT-e HALL-ten

425. That's more than what's on the meter.
Das ist mehr als der Taxometer anzeigt.
dass ist MAIR als dair TAKS-owe-may-tah AN-tseigt

426. I don't have any smaller bills.   *Ich hab's nicht kleiner.*
isch HABS nischt kline-ah

427. Keep the change.   *Stimmt schon.*   **SHTIMT shawn**

TAKING THE SUBWAY

428. Subway.   *Die U-Bahn.*   **dee OO-bahn**

429. A subway ticket.   *Ein Fahrschein für die U-Bahn.*
Ein FAHR-shine fewr dee OO-bahn

430. Where is the closest subway station?
Wo ist die nächste U-Bahnstation?
VOH ist dee naykh-ste OO-bahn shtat-tsee-ohn

431. Where is the subway map?
Wo ist der Fahrplan für die U-Bahn?
VOH ist dair FAHR-plahn FEWR dee OO-bahn?

432. Which line do I take to go to _____?
Welche Linie geht nach _____?
VEL-sche LEE-nee-e gait nakh

433. I'd like a day ticket, please.
Ich möchte bitte eine Tageskarte.
isch MEWSH-te BIT-e ein-e-TAG-ess-kar-te

434. Is this the subway train to Schwabing?
Ist das die U-Bahn nach Schwabing?
IST dass dee OO-bahn nakh SHVAH-bing?

435. Can I change at Marienplatz?
Kann ich am Marienplatz umsteigen?
KANN isch am mah-REE-en-PLATS OOM-shteig-en?

436. What is the next stop?
      Wo ist die nächste Haltestelle?
      VOH ist die naykhs-te HALL-te-shte-le

TRAVELING ON TWO WHEELS

437. Bicycle.   *Das (Fahr)rad.*   **dass (FAHR)-raht**

438. I'm planning on riding my bike this morning.
      Ich will heute morgen mit dem Rad fahren.
      ISCH vill HOY-te MOR-gen mit daym RAHT FAH-ren

439. Do you have a bike helmet?
      Haben Sie einen Fahrradhelm? (formal, singular or plural)
      HA-ben zee ein-en FAHR-raht-helm

      Habt ihr einen Fahrradhelm? (informal, plural)
      HABT EE-ah ein-en FAHR-rat-helm

      Hast du einen Fahrradhelm? (informal, singular)
      HAST doo ein-en FAHR-rat-helm

440. I would like to rent a bike.   *Ich möchte ein Fahrrad mieten.*
      isch MEWSH-te ein FAHR-rat MEET-en

441. Are there bike paths?   *Gibt es hier Fahrradwege?*
      GIPT ess hee-ah FAHR-rat-VAY-ge?

442. Scooter.   *Ein Motorroller.*   **EIN mow-TOR-roll-ah**

443. I'd like to rent a scooter.
      Ich möchte einen Motorroller mieten.
      isch MEWSH-te EIN-nen mow-TOR-roll-e MEET-en

TRAVELING ON FOOT

444. Can I get there on foot?   *Kann ich zu Fuß dahin gehen?*
      KANN isch tsoo FOOSS da-HIN GAY-en?

445. It's ten minutes away.
      Es sind vielleicht zehn Minuten bis dahin.
      ESS zint feel-EISHT TSAIN mi-NOOT-en biss da-HIN

446. Do you have a map of the neighborhood?
Haben Sie eine Karte von diesem Stadtviertel?
HA-ben zee ein-e KAR-te fawn dee-zem SHTAT-feer-tl?

447. Can you recommend a guided walk?
Können Sie eine Stadtführung empfehlen? (formal, singular or plural)
KOENN-en ZEE ein-e SHTAT-FEWR-oong emp-FAY-len

Könnt ihr eine Stadtführung empfehlen? (informal, plural)
KOENNT EE-ah ein-e SHTAT-fewr-oong emp-FAY-len

Kannst du eine Stadtführung empfehlen? (informal)
KANNST doo ein-e SHTAT-fewr-oong emp-FAY-len

448. Do you have a guide to local walks?
Haben Sie eine Karte für die Wanderwege in der Gegend? (formal, singular or plural)
HA-ben ZEE ein-e KAR-te fewr dee VAN-de-vay-ga IN dair GAY-gent

Habt ihr eine Karte für die Wanderwege in der Gegend? (informal, plural)
HABT EE-ah EIN-e KAR-te fewr dee VAN-de-VAY-ge IN dair-GAY-gent

Hast du eine Karte für die Wanderwege in der Gegend? (informal, singular)
HAST doo EIN-e KAR-te fewr dee VAN-de-VAY-ge IN dair GAY-gent

449. How long will this walk take?
Wie lange dauert dieser Spaziergang?
vee LANG-e DOW-aht DEE-zer shpats-EER-gahng

450. We'd like to take a hike.
Wir möchten eine Wanderung machen.
VEE-ah MEWHS-ten EIN-e VAN-de-roong makh-en

451. We'd like to go climbing.   *Wir möchten klettern gehen.*
VEE-ah MEWHS-ten KLET-ern GAY-en

452. Do I need walking shoes?   *Soll ich Wanderschuhe anziehen?*
ZAUL isch VAN-de-shoo-e AN-tsee-en

453. Where are the hiking trails?   *Wo sind die Wanderwege?*
VOH zint dee VAN-de-VAY-ge

454. Is it a difficult climb?   *Ist das ein schwerer Aufstieg?*
IST dass ein SHVE-rah AUF-shteek

455. Is it steep?   *Ist es ein steiler Aufstieg?*
IST es ein SHTILE-ah AUF-shteek

AT THE HOTEL

456. Can you suggest _____?
Können Sie _____ empfehlen? (formal, singular or plural)
KOENN-en ZEE _____ -emp-FAIL-en

    Könnt ihr _____ empfehlen? (informal, plural)
KOENT EE-ah _____ -emp-FAIL-en

    Kannst du _____ empfehlen? (informal, singular)
KANNST doo _____ -emp-FAIL-en

    _____ a good hotel?   _____ ein gutes Hotel?
ein GOOT-es hoh-TELL

    _____ an inexpensive hotel?
_____ *ein günstiges Hotel.*
EIN GUENST-ig-es hoh-TELL

457. Do you have a vacancy?   *Haben Sie Zimmer?*
HA-ben ZEE TSIMM-ah

458. I'd like a double room.   *Ich möche ein Doppelzimmer.*
ISCH MEWSH-te EIN DOPP-ell-TSIMM-ah

459. I'd like a room for one person.
Ich möchte ein Einbettzimmer.
ISCH MEWSH-te ein EIN-bett-TSIMM-ah

460. I'd like a room with two beds.
Ich möchte ein Zimmer mit zwei Einzelbetten.
ISCH MEWSH-te ein TSIMM-ah mit TSVEYE EIN-tsel-bett-en

461. I have a reservation under the name of _____.
Ich habe eine Reservierung für _____.
ISCH HA-be ein-e re-ze-VEER-oong fewr

462. Where can I park the car?   *Wo kann ich mein Auto parken?*
VOH KAUNN isch mine AU-toh PARK-en

463. For two nights.   *Für zwei Nächte.*
fewr TSVEYE NAEKH-te

464. May I see the room?   *Kann ich das Zimmer sehen?*
KANN isch dass TSIMM-ah ZAY-en

465. Would it be possible to have another room?
Kann ich bitte ein anderes Zimmer haben?
KANN isch BIT-e ein AN-de-res TSIMM-ah HA-ben?

466. Is breakfast included in the price?
Ist der Preis inclusive Frühstück?
IST dair PREIS IN-kloo-ZEE-ve FREW-stuek?

467. Does the room have _____?
Hat das Zimmer _____?
HAT dass TSIMM-ah

_____ a shower?   _____ *eine Dusche?*
ein-e DOOSH-e

_____ a bath?   _____ *ein Bad?*   ein BAHT

_____ a TV?   _____ *einen Fernseher?*
EIN-en FERN-zay-ah

_____ a high-speed Internet connection?
_____ *einen Hochgeschwindigkeitsinternetanschluss?*
ein-en HOKH-ge-shvinn-disch-kites-IN-tah-net-AN-
shlooss

_____ air conditioning?   _____ *eine Klimaanlage?*
ein-e KLEE-mah-AN-LA-ge

468. May I have the key?   *Kann ich die Schlüssel haben?*
KANN isch dee SHLEWSS-l HA-ben

469. We'll be back after midnight.
Wir sind nach Mitternacht zurück.
VEE-ah ZINT nakh MIT-e-nakht tsoo-REWK

470. Will the door be locked?   *Ist die Tür abgeschlossen?*
IST dee TEWR AP-ge-shloss-en?

471. Will we need to ring the bell?   *Müssen wir klingeln?*
MEWS-en vee-ah KLING-eln

Chapter 3
Mealtimes

How people talk about mealtimes may vary in German-speaking countries. In all German-speaking countries die Mahlzeiten (meals) consist of das Frühstück (breakfast), das Mittagessen (lunch) and das Abendessen (dinner). In Austria, a Jause (a meal or snack consisting of bread, cold cuts, and cheese, or sometimes even a layer cake or a piece of strudel) is added to the meal choices, usually between breakfast and lunch or in the evening. Similarly, in Bavaria there is a mid-morning or late-afternoon meal called "Brotzeit." In Switzerland, a late-afternoon snack at about four o'clock called Zvieri is composed of sausages or ham with pickles and bread served with hard cider or beer. For those who prefer lighter eating, the Zvieri might consist of bread and butter, served either with Milchkaffee (café au lait) or tea. For those with a sweeter tooth, simple cakes or buns are an alternative.

Germans throughout the country like to have a Kaffeklatsch (literally, coffee gossip), either at home or in one of the many Konditoreien (pastry shops) and Kaffeehäuser (coffee houses) that offer mouthwatering pastries, cookies, layer cakes, strudels, éclairs, and more). Austria, and its capital, Vienna, in particular, is famous for its long-standing and ritualized Kaffeehaus tradition. Viennese people can spend hours in a Kaffeehaus, reading the paper, composing letters and poems, or enjoying one of the many dishes offered.

Lunch and dinner are fairly similar affairs in all German-speaking countries, either consisting of meat, a side dish such as potatoes, dumplings or rice, or sausages and potato salad with sauerkraut. Where the tradition still calls for a large lunch, dinner is considerably smaller.

The cuisine of northern Germany is greatly influenced by its proximity to the Scandinavian countries and the Netherlands. Due to the damp, cold climate, northern Germans have a taste for thick soups, pickled and smoked meats and fish, dried fruits, smoked bacon, sour cream, and many dishes containing goose meat and eel. One famous delicacy is the Labskaus: a one-dish meal of meat and fish plus vegetables that originated as a sailor's specialty. A favorite throughout Germany is the Schlachtplatte, literally "slaughter plate," with its variety of meats and sausages served with bread, pickles, and cold beer.

Don't leave Switzerland without enjoying either one of the gastronomic masterpieces Swiss cuisine is famous for namely, the raclette and the cheese fondue. The former consists of mountain cheese melted before a special heater or an open fire and served with a crunchy sweet pickled gherkin and a few pickled onions. The final touch in both flavor and texture is a boiled potato. A cheese fondue is essentially cheese melted in wine or cider and lightly seasoned with garlic and a splash of Kirsch (cherry schnapps). Diners dip chunks of crusty bread into the melted cheese mixture. At the end of the meal, a tasty crust of cheese will have formed at the bottom of the pot which is served to all, together with hot tea to complete the fondue dinner.

TALKING ABOUT MEALTIMES AND EATING: GENERAL EXPRESSIONS

472. Breakfast.   *Das Frühstück.*   **dass FREW-SHTUEK**

Lunch.   *Das Mittagessen.*   **dass MIT-ak-ESS-en**

Dinner.   *Das Abendessen.*   **dass AH-bent-ESS-en**

Dessert.   *Die Nachspeise.*   **dee NAKH-shpeye-ze**

The mid-morning or mid-afternoon snack.

Die Brotzeit (Bavaria).   **dee BROHT-tsite**

Die Jause (Austria).   **dee YOW-ze**

Das Zvierie (Switzerland).   **dass TSVEE-ree**

The mid-afternoon snack (sweet).

Der Kaffeeklatsch.   **dair KAFF-aye-KLATSH**

473. I'm (very) hungry.   *Ich bin (sehr) hungrig.*
ISCH bin (ZAIR) HOONG-risch

474. I'm not (very) hungry.   *Ich bin nicht (sehr) hungrig.*
ISCH bin NISCHT (ZAIR) HOONG-risch

475. I'm dying of hunger!   *Ich bin am Verhungern!*
ISCH bin AM fe-HOONG-an

476. Would you like more _____?
     Möchten Sie noch etwas _____?
     MEWSH-ten ZEE nokh ET-VASS

     _____ salad?   _____ *Salat?*   **za-LAWT**

     _____ chicken?   _____ *Hähnchen?*   **HAEN-schyen**

     _____ meat?   _____ *Fleisch?*   **FLYSH**

     _____ beer?   _____ *Bier?*   **BEE-ah**

     _____ wine?   _____ *Wein?*   **VINE**

     _____ coffee?   _____ *Kaffee?*   **KAFF-aye**

     _____ dessert?   _____ *Nachspeise?*
     NAKH-shpeye-ze

477. No thanks, I'm full.   *Nein, danke. Ich bin satt.*
     nine DAN-ke isch bin ZATT

478. Yes, just a little, thanks.   *Ja, noch ein bisschen, bitte.*
     YAH NOKH ein BISS-chyen BIT- e

479. Enjoy your meal!   *Guten Appetit!*   **GOO-ten AP-e-TEET**

480. It's delicious.   *Es schmeckt köstlich.*
     ESS shmeckt KOEST-lisch

481. Cheers!   *Zum Wohl! (formal)*   **tsoom VOL**
     Prost! (semi-formal)   **PROHST**

482. I'm a vegetarian.   *Ich bin _____.*   **ISCH bin**

     _____ *Vegetarier. (masc)*   **VE-ge-TAHR-ee-ah**

     _____ *Vegetarierin (f.)*   **VE-ge-TAHR-ee-ah-rin**

483. A food allergy.   *Eine Lebensmittelallergie.*
     EIN-e LAY-bens-MIT-l-AL-er-GHEE

484. I'm allergic _____.   *Ich bin _____ allergisch.*
     isch bin al-AIR-gish

485. _____ to peanut products.
     _____ *gegen Erdnußprodukte _____.*
     GAY-gen ERD-nousse-proh-DOUK-te

486. _____ to seafood.
      _____ *gegen Meeresfrüchte* _____.
           GAY-gen MAIR-es-froosh-te

487. I'm lactose intolerant.
      Ich habe eine Milchzuckerunverträglichkeit.
      ISCH HA-be ein-e MILSCH-tsook-er-OUN-fa-
      TRAYG-lisch-kite

488. I'm on a diet.   *Ich mache eine Diät.*
      ISCH MAKH-e ein-e dee-AIT

DINING OUT

489. Can you suggest _____?
      Können Sie _____ empfehlen? (formal, singular or plural)
      KOENN-en ZEE-_____-em-FAY-len

      Könnt ihr _____ empfehlen? (informal, plural)
      KOENNT EE-ah-_____-em-FAY-len

      Kannst du _____ empfehlen? (informal, singular)
      KANNST doo-_____-em-FAY-len

490. _____ a good restaurant?
      _____ *ein gutes Restaurant* _____?
           EIN GOOT-es ress-tau-RAHN

491. _____ something close by?
      _____ *etwas in der Nähe* _____?
           ET-vass IN dair NAY-e?

492. _____ a cheap restaurant?
      _____ *ein preiswertes Restaurant* _____?
           EIN PREIS-vert es ress-tau-RAHN

493. I like _____ cuisine.   *Ich liebe die _____ Küche.*
      isch LEE-be dee_____KUESCH-e

      _____ German_____.   _____ *deutsche* _____.
      DOITSH-e

      _____ regional_____.   _____ *regionale* _____.
      RAY-ghee-own-AHL-e

_____ Italian _____.   _____ *italienische* _____.
Ih-tahl-ee-YAYN-ish-e

_____ Spanish _____.   _____ *spanische* _____.
SHPAH-ni-she

_____ Moroccan_____.
_____ *marokkanische* _____.
MAH-row-KAHN-i-sch-e

_____ Indian _____.   _____ *indische* _____.
IN-disch-e

_____ vegetarian_____.
_____ *vegetarische* _____.
ve-ge-TAHR-isch-e

494. We're looking for_____.   *Wir suchen* _____.
VEE-ah SOOKH-n

_____ a café.   _____ *ein Café.*   **ein kah-FAY**

_____ a snack bar.   _____ *einen Schnellimbiss.*
EIN-en SHNELL-im-biss

_____ a bar.   _____ *eine Bar.*   **EIN-e BAHR**

_____ a restaurant.   _____ *ein Restaurant.*
EIN ress-tau-RAHN

_____ a pastry shop.   _____ *eine Konditorei.*
EIN-e kon-di-toh-RYE

_____ a deli.   _____ *einen Delikatessenladen.*
EIN-en dell-ee-kah-TESS-en-LAH-den

495. I'd like to reserve a table _____.
Ich möchte einen Tisch _____ *reservieren.*
ISCH MEWSH-te EIN-en TISCH _____ **re-ze-VEER-en**

_____ for two _____.   _____ *für zwei.*
fewr TSVEYE

_____ for tonight_____.   _____ *für heute Abend.*
fewr HOYT-e AH-bent

_____ for tomorrow night_____.
_____ *für morgen Abend.*   **fewr MOR-gen AH-bent**

496. May I see the menu, please?
Kann ich bitte die Speisekarte sehen?
KANN isch BIT-e dee SHPIZE-e-KAR-te ZAY-en

497.   What do you recommend _____?
       Was empfehlen Sie _____?
       VASS em-FAY-len ZEE

       _____ as an appetizer?   _____ *als Vorspeise?*
       ALS FAW-shpize-e

       _____ as a main course?   _____ *als Hauptgang?*
       ALS HAUPT-gang

       _____ as a side dish?   _____ *als Beilage?*
       ALS BYE-la-ge

       _____ as a dessert?   _____ *als Nachspeise?*
       ALS NAKH-shpize-e

498.   I'll have_____.   *Ich nehme_____.*   **ISCH NAY-meh**

       _____ the tourist menu.   _____ *das Touristenmenü.*
       dass tu-RIST-en me-NEW

       . . . the fixed-priced menu.
       _____ *das Menü von der Tageskarte.*
       dass me-NEW fawn dair TAH-guess-KAR-te

499.   Enjoy your meal!   *Guten Appetit!*   **GOO-ten AH-pe-TEET**

500.   Thanks, same to you!   *Danke, gleichfalls!*
       DAN-ke GLYSCH-falls

501.   It's _____.   *Es ist_____.*   **ESS IST**

       _____ too salty.   _____ *versalzt.*   **feah-ZALTST**

       _____ too spicy.   _____ *verwürzt.*
       feah-VEWTST

       _____ sour.   _____ *sauer.*   **SAU-ah**

       _____ bitter.   _____ *bitter.*   **BIT-ah**

502.   It's not _____ enough.   *Es ist nicht _____ genug.*
       Ess ist nischt ge-NOOK

       _____ sweet_____.   _____ *süß_____.*   **SEWSS**

       _____ hot_____.   _____ *scharf_____.*   **SHARF**

503.   It's a bit tasteless.   *Es schmeckt ein bisschen fade.*
       ESS SHMECKT ein BISS-schen FAH-de

504.   More _____, please.   *Mehr _____, bitte.*
       MAY-ah _____ BIT-e

_____ bread_____.   _____ Brot_____.
BROHT

_____ water_____.   _____ Mineralwasser_____.
MI-ne-RAL-vass-ah

505. The bill, please.   *Die Rechnung, bitte.*
dee RESCH-noong BIT-e

506. Is the tip included?   *Ist das Trinkgeld im Preis einbegriffen?*
IST dass TRINK-gelt im PREIS EIN-be-GRIFF-en?

MENU: GENERAL ITEMS

507. Bread.   *Das Brot.*   **dass BROHT**

508. Roll.   *Das Brötchen.*   **dass BREWT-schen**

509. Toast.   *Der Toast.*   **dair TOHST**

510. Salt.   *Das Salz.*   **dass ZALTS**

511. Pepper.   *Der Pfeffer.*   **dair PFEFF-ah**

512. Butter.   *Die Butter.*   **dee BOOT-ah**

513. Sugar.   *Der Zucker.*   **dair TSOOK-ah**

514. Cinnamon.   *Der Zimt.*   **dair TSIMT**

515. Vinaigrette dressing.   *Die Vinaigrette.*   **dee vi-nah-GRETT**

516. Tap water.   *Das Leitungswasser.*   **dass LITE-oongs-vass-ah**

517. Mineral water (non-carbonated).   *Das stille Mineralwasser.*
dass SHTILL-e minn-e-RAHL-vass-ah

518. Sparkling water.   *Der Sprudel.*   **dair SHPROO-dl**

519. With ice.   *mit Eis.*   **mit ICE**

520. Mustard.   *Der Senf.*   **dair ZENF**

521. Garlic.   *Der Knoblauch.*   **dair KNOH-blaukh**

BREAKFAST FOOD

Breakfast in Germany is a serious matter. Germans like a hearty breakfast, and it's simply too delicious to skip. It pays to look for accommodation that includes a breakfast buffet: "Frühstück inbegriffen." Usually, the larger the hotel, the more diverse the breakfast selection. However, even a smaller hotel or a family-run "Gasthaus" (inn) will usually provide a very decent breakfast. The advantage of a large breakfast is that you don't have to spend so much for lunch, or you can even skip it altogether.

The breakfast choices include bacon, sausage, ham, cold cuts, eggs, cereals, cheeses, marmalades, jellies, jams, and fruits, along with a selection of German breads, including rolls made with seeds and nuts, whole-grain or white. Are you hungry yet? Some top-flight hotels also offer fresh tomatoes or other seasonal vegetables, exotic fruits, and cold meats and fish, such as chicken, roast beef, or smoked salmon.

So, develop an appetite for breakfast and start practicing your German! In the end, after you've enjoyed your breakfast, you might want to pay a compliment to the server or manager by saying, "das Essen war sehr gut!"

522. I'll have _____.   *Ich nehme _____.*   **isch NAY-me**

_____ coffee.   _____ *einen Kaffee.*   **EIN-en kaff-AYE**

_____ coffee with cream.

_____ *einen Kaffee mit Milch.*
EIN-en kaff-AYE mit MILSCH

_____ decaf.   _____ *einen Kaffee ohne Koffein.*
EIN-en kaff-AYE OHN-e koff-aye-EEN

523. We'd like_____.   *Wir möchten _____.*
VEER MEWSH-ten

_____ large coffee with frothy milk.
_____ *einen grossen Kaffee mit schaumiger Milch.*
EIN-en GROSS-en kaff-AYE mit SHAU-mee-ge gah MILSCH

524. In the mornings I have _____.
Morgens trinke ich _____.
MOR-gens TRINK-e isch

_____ Tea with lemon.   _____ *Tee mit Zitrone.*
TAY mit tsi-TROH-ne

_____ Tea with milk.   _____ *Tee mit Milch.*
TAY mit MILSCH

525. Do you want _____?
Möchten Sie _____? (formal, singular or plural)
MEWSH-ten ZEE

Möchtet ihr _____? (informal, plural)
MEWSH-tet EE-ah

Möchtest du _____? (informal, singular)
MEWSH-test doo

_____ hot chocolate.   _____ *eine heiße Schokolade.*
EIN-e hi-se shok-o-LAH-de

526. I would rather have _____.
Ich möchte lieber _____.
ISCH MEWSH-te LEE-bah

_____ A glass of fruit juice.   _____ *einen Fruchtsaft.*
EIN-en FROOSCHT-zaft

_____ A glass of orange juice.
_____ *einen Orangensaft.*
EIN-en aw-RANG-zhen-zaft

527. I would like some toast _____, please.
Ich möchte bitte etwas Toast _____.
ISCH MEWSH-te BIT-e ET-vass TOHST

_____ with jam.   _____ *mit Marmelade.*
mit mar-me-LAH-de

_____ with honey.   _____ *mit Honig.*   **mit HOH-nisch**

I would like _____.   *Ich möchte bitte _____.*
ISCH MEWSH-BIT- e

_____ some cereal.   _____ *Frühstücksflocken/Müsli.*
FREW-shtooks-FLAW-ken/MEWS-lee

_____ an egg.   _____ *ein Ei.*   **EIN EYE**

_____ some fried eggs.   _____ *Spiegeleier.*
SPEE-gl-EYE-ah

_____ scrambled eggs.   _____ *Rühreier.*
REWAH-EYE-ah

_____ an omelet.   _____ *ein Omelett.*
EIN om-LET

_____ a soft-boiled egg.   _____ *ein weiches Ei.*
EIN VAI-sches EYE

_____ a cheese omelet.   _____ *ein Omelett mit Käse.*
EIN om-LET mit KAY-ze

_____ bacon and eggs.   _____ *Eier mit Speck.*
EYE-ah mit SHPEK

_____ ham and eggs.   _____ *Eier mit Schinken.*
EYE-ah mit SHIN-ken

_____ a yogurt.   _____ *ein Joghurt.*
EIN YOH-goort

_____ breakfast pastries.   _____ *Backwaren.*
BAK-vah-ren

_____ a croissant.
_____ *ein Blätterteighörnchen. Hörnchen.*
EIN BLAETT-ah-teig-HOERN-schen HOERN-schen

_____ a chocolate-filled croissant.
_____ *ein Schokoladenhörnchen.*
EIN shok-oh-LAH-den-HOERN-schen

_____ a raisin bun.   _____ *eine Rosinenschnecke.*
EIN-e roh-ZEE-nen-SHNECK-e

APPETIZERS, LUNCH ITEMS AND SALAD

528. We'd like to have a light meal.
Wir möchten eine leichte Mahlzeit.
VEE-ah MEWSH-ten EIN-e LEYE-shteh MAHL-tsite

529. Soup. *Die Suppe.* **dee ZOOP-e**

530. Chicken noodle soup. *Die Hühnernudelsuppe.*
dee HEWN-ah-NOO-dell-ZOOP-e

531. Vegetable soup. *Die Gemüseseuppe.*
dee ge-MEWZ-e-ZOOP-e

532. German potato soup. *Die deutsche Kartoffelsuppe.*
dee DOITSH-e kar-TOFF-ell-ZOOP-e

533. Eel soup. `*Die Aalsuppe.* **dee AHL-ZOOP-e**

534. Plate of cold meat.   *Die kalte Platte.*   **dee KAL-te PLAT-e**

535. I feel like having _____.   *Ich habe Lust auf _____.*
      ISCH HA-be LOOST auf

      _____ A sandwich.   _____ *Ein belegtes Brot.*
      EIN be-LAYG-tes BROHT

      _____ A ham sandwich.   _____ *Ein Schinkenbrot.*
      ein SHINK-en-BROHT

      _____ A tuna sandwich.   _____ *Ein Thunfischbrot.*
      ein TOON-fish-BROHT

      _____ A cheese sandwich.   _____ *Ein Käsebrot.*
      ein KAY-zuh-BROHT

      _____ brats on a roll.   _____ *ein Bratwurstbrötchen.*
      ein BRAHT-voorst BREWT-schen

      _____ brats with curry on a roll.
      _____ *eine Currywurst.*
      EIN-e CURR-ee-VOORST

      _____ A pair of sausages with mustard and potato salad.
      _____ *ein Paar Wienerwürstchen mit Senf und
      Kartoffelsalat.*
      **ein PAHR VEE-nah-VOORST-schen MIT ZENF
      oont kar-TOFF-ell-za-LAHT**

536. He /She will have _____.   *Er/sie nimmt _____.*
      E-ah/ZEE NIMMT

      _____ A casserole.   _____ *einen Auflauf.*
      EIN-en AUF-lauf

      _____ A green salad.   _____ *einen grünen Salat.*
      EIN-en GREWN-en za-LAHT

      _____ A mixed salad.   _____ *einen gemischten Salat.*
      EIN-en ge-MISH-ten za-LAHT

      _____ A cucumber salad.   _____ *einen Gurkensalat.*
      EIN-en GOOR-ken-za-LAHT

      _____ A tomato salad.   _____ *einen Tomatensalat.*
      EIN-en toh-MA-ten-za-LAHT

      _____ French fries with ketchup and mayonnaise.
      _____ *Pommes Frittes mit Ketchup und Mayo.*
      pomm-FRITS mit KETSH-up oont MAY-oh

MAIN COURSE

537. We'd like to eat _____.   *Wir möchten* _____ *essen.*
Vee-ah MEWSH-ten _____ESS-en

_____ now.   _____ *jetzt* _____.   **YETST**

_____ later.   _____ *später* _____.   **SHPAY-tah**

538. I'm ordering _____.   *Ich möchte* _____.
ish MEWSH-te _____

_____ Some roast chicken.   _____ *ein Brathähnchen.*
EIN BRAHT-haen-schen

_____ Some grilled fish.   _____ *gegrillten Fisch.*
ge-GRILL-ten FISH

_____ Some salmon.   _____ *Lachs.*   **LAKS**

539. I like _____.   *Ich mag* _____ *sehr gern.*
ish MAHK _____ZAIR geahn

_____ Seafood.   _____ *Meeresfrüchte* _____.
MAIR-es-FREWSH-te

_____ Mussels.   _____ *Muscheln* _____.
MOOSH-eln

_____ Crab.   _____ *Krebse* _____.   **KRAYB-se**

_____ Shrimp.   _____ *Krabben* _____.   **KRAB-en**

_____ Lobster.   _____ *Hummer* _____.
HOOM-ah

_____ Oysters.   _____ *Austern* _____.   **AU-stahn**

540. I'm not too fond of . . .   *Ich mag* _____ *nicht so gern.*
isch MAHG _____ NISCHT zoh geahn

_____ Steak.   _____ *Steak* _____.   **SHTAYK**

_____ Leg of lamb.   _____ *Lammkeule* _____.
LAMM-koy-le

_____ Pork.   _____ *Schweinefleisch* _____.
SHVINE-e-FLEISH

_____ Ham.   _____ *Schinken* _____.   **SHIHNK-en**

541. I rarely eat _____.   *Ich esse selten _____.*
     isch ESS-e ZELL-ten

     _____ Veal.   _____ *Kalbfleisch.*   **KALP-fleish**

     _____ Roast beef.   _____ *Rindfleisch.*   **RINT-fleish**

     _____ A filet of turkey.   _____ *Truthahnbrust.*
     TROOT-hahn-broost

542. Pasta.   *Nudelgerichte.*   **NOOD-l-ge-RISHT-te**

543. Choice of vegetable.   *Gemüse nach Wahl.*
     ge-MEWZ-e nakh VAHL

544. A vegetarian dish.   *Ein vegetarisches Gericht.*
     EIN ve-ge-TAR-ish-es ge-RISCHT

545. Stew.   *Der Eintopf.*   **dair EIN-topf**

546. Rice.   *Der Reis.*   **dair REIS**

FRUITS AND VEGETABLES

547. If I'm a little hungry I eat _____.
     Für den kleinen Hunger esse ich _____.
     Fewr dayn KLEIN-en HOONG-er ESS-e isch

     _____ An apple.   _____ *Einen Apfel.*   **EIN-en APF-l**

     _____ An orange.   _____ *Eine Orange.*
     EIN-e o-RANGSH-e

     _____ A grapefruit.   _____ *Eine Grapefruit.*
     EIN-e GRAHP-frewt

     _____ A pear.   _____ *Eine Birne.*   **EIN-e BIR-ne**

     _____ A banana.   _____ *Eine Banane.*
     EIN-e ba-NAH-ne

548. Can I give you _____.
     Kann ich Ihnen _____ geben? (formal, singular or plural)
     KANN isch EE-nen _____ GAY-ben

     Kann ich euch _____ geben? (informal, plural)
     KANN isch OISH _____ GAY-ben

     Kann ich dir _____ geben? (informal, singular)
     KANN isch DEE-ah _____ GAY-ben

_____ Some cherries.   _____ *Kirschen* _____.
KEARSH-en

_____ Some grapes.   _____ *Weintrauben.*
VINE-trau-ben

_____ Some strawberries.   _____ *Erdbeeren* _____.
ERT-bear-en

549. I need _____.   *Ich brauche* _____.   **isch BRAU-khe**

_____ A lemon.   _____ *Eine Zitrone.*
EIN-e tsi-TROH-ne

_____ A lime.   _____ *Eine Limone.*
EIN-e li-MOH-ne

_____ A peach.   _____ *Einen Pfirsich.*
EIN-en PFIR-zisch

550. _____ A fruit salad.   _____ *Einen Fruchtsalat.*
EIN-en FROOSCHT-za-laht

_____ A green salad.   _____ *Einen grünen Salat.*
EIN-en GREWN-en za-laht

551. I'd like to buy _____.   *Ich möchte* _____ *kaufen.*
isch mewsh-te _____ KAU-fen.

_____ Some carrots.   _____ *Etwas Karotten.*
ET-vas ka-ROTT-en

_____ Some roasted potatoes.
_____ *Etwas Bratkartoffeln* _____.
ET-vas BRAHT-kar-TOFF-eln

_____ Some mashed potatoes.
_____ *Etwas Kartoffelbrei* _____.
ET-vas kar-TOFF-el-brye

_____ Some potato salad.
_____ *Kartoffelsalat* _____.
kar-TOFF-el-za-laht

_____ Some tomato salad.   _____ *Etwas Tomatensalat.*
ET-vas toh-MA-ten-za-laht

_____ Some lettuce.   _____ *Etwas Grünen Salat.*
ET-vas GREW-nen za-laht

_____ Some zucchini.   _____ *Etwas Zucchini.*
ET-vas tsoo-KEE-nee

_____ Some parsley.   _____ *Etwas Petersilie.*
ET-vas PE-tah-ZAY-lee-e

_____ Some chives.   _____ *Etwas Schnittlauch.*
ET-vas SHNIT-laukh

_____ Some cauliflower.   _____ *Etwas Blumenkohl.*
ET-vas BLOO-men-kohl

552. To make a salad, I'll need to buy _____.
Für einen Salat brauche ich _____.
FEWR EIN-en za-LAHT BROW-khe isch

_____ Some green peppers.
_____ *Etwas grüne Paprika.*
ET-vas GREW-ne PAP-ree-kah

_____ Some mushrooms.
_____ *Etwas Champignons.*   **ET-vas SHAM-pin-yons**

_____ Some spinach.   _____ *Etwas Spinat.*
ET-vas SPHI-naht

_____ Some cucumbers.   _____ *Etwas Gurken.*
ET-vas GOOR-ken

_____ Some leeks.   _____ *Etwas Lauch.*
ET-vas LAUKH

DESSERT

In all German-speaking countries, desserts are served as part of a meal such as lunch or dinner or constitute the main feature in the afternoon snack, the "Kaffeeklatsch" or "Zvierie." A wide variety of "Kuchen," "Torten," "Strudel," and other pastries are served on these occasions, most commonly made with fresh fruit. Apples, plums, strawberries, blueberries, and cherries are used regularly in cakes and strudels. "Käsekuchen," or cheesecake, is also very popular, often made with Quark, a kind of curd cheese, and fresh cream. Schwarzwälder Kirschtorte, Black Forest cake, made with cherries, is one of the bright stars in the layer-cake constellation, as is Sachertorte, Sacher cake, made with a peach-jelly filling.

German doughnuts are made of yeast dough with jam or other fillings and are known as "Berliner," "Kreppel" or "Krapfen," depending on the region. "Eierkuchen" or "Pfannkuchen" are large and thin pancakes, comparable to French crèpes. They are covered with sugar, jam or syrup. In some regions, "Eierkuchen" are filled and then wrapped; in Austria and southern Germany, they are baked in the oven, cut into small pieces and arranged in a heap, called "Kaiserschmarrn."

In northern Germany, "Rote Grütze," a kind of red fruit pudding made with berries and cherries, then cooked in jelly and served with cream, vanilla sauce, milk or whipped cream, is very popular. Variations on the theme are "Rhabarbergrütze" (rhubarb pudding) and "Grüne Grütze" (gooseberry pudding). Germans are also fond of "Fruchtsalat" (fruit salad), ice cream, or sorbets for dessert. Italian-run ice cream parlors, found on every corner in the summer, serve the best ice cream in Germany, and "Pistazie" (pistachio), "Stracciatella" (whipped frozen cream with chocolate chunks), and "Spaghetti" (vanilla ice cream with strawberry syrup) are among the favorite flavors.

553. What would you like for dessert?
Was möchten Sie als Nachspeise? (formal, singular or plural)
vass MEWSH-ten-ZEE als NAKH-shpy-ze

Was möchtet ihr als Nachspeise? (informal, plural)
vass MEWSH-tet EE-ah als NAKH-shpy-ze

Was möchtest du als Nachspeise? (informal, singular)
vass MEWSH-test DOO als NAKH-shpy-ze

554. What desserts do you have?
Was für Nachspeisen haben Sie? (formal, singular or plural)
vass FEWR NAKH-shpy-zen HA-ben ZEE

Was für Nachspeisen habt ihr? (informal, plural)
vass FEWR NAKH-shpy-zen HAHBT EE-ah

Was für Nachspeisen haben Sie? (informal, singular)
vass FEWR NAKH-shpy-zen HAST doo

555. Can you suggest _____.
Was für _____ können Sie empfehlen? (formal)
VASS fewr_____ KOENN-en ZEE emp-FAY-len

_____ fruit?   _____ *Obst* _____?   **OHBST**

_____ strudel?   _____ *einen Strudel* _____?
SHTROO-dl?

_____ a cake?   _____ *einen Kuchen* _____?
EIN-en KOO-khen

_____ a layer cake?   _____ *eine Torte*_____?
EIN-e TOR-te

_____ Ice cream?   _____ *Eis* _____?   **ICE**

We would like a different type of dessert.
Wir möchten eine andere Nachspeise.
VEE-ah MEWSH-ten EIN-e AN-de-re NAKH-shpy-ze

556.   What would you like instead?   *Und was hätten Sie gern?*
OONT vass HETT-en ZEE geahrn

557.   Chocolate cake.   *Schokoladenkuchen.*
SHOK-oh-LAH-den-KOO-KHEN

558.   ice cream.   *Eis.*   **ICE**

559.   vanilla ice cream.   *Vanilleeis.*   **va-NEE-ah-ICE**

560.   Some apple pie.   *Apfelkuchen.*   **APF-el-KOO-khen**

561.   Some Strudel.   *Strudel.*   **SHTROO-dl**

562.   A piece of layer cake.   *Ein Stück Torte.*   **EIN shtook TOR-te**

BEVERAGES

563.   Would you like to have a drink?
Möchten Sie etwas trinken? (formal, singular or plural)
MEWSH-ten zee ET-vas TRIN-ken

Möchtet ihr etwas trinken? (informal, plural)
MEWSH-tet EE-ah ET-vas TRIN-ken

Möchtest du etwas trinken? (informal, singular)
MEWSH-test DOO ET-vas TRIN-ken

564.   What would you like?
Was möchten Sie? (formal, singular or plural)
VAS MEWSH-ten ZEE

Was möchtet ihr? (informal, plural)
VAS MEWSH-tet EE-ah

Was möchtest du? (informal, singular)
VAS MEWSH-test DOO

565.   I'll get it!   *Ich zahle!*   **ISCH TSAH-le**

566.   I'm buying this round of drinks.   *Diese Runde zahle ich!*
DEE-ze ROON-de TSAH-le ISCH

567. The wine list, please.   *Die Weinkarte, bitte.*
    dee VINE-ka-te BIT-e

568. A bottle of wine.   *Eine Flasche Wein, bitte.*
    EIN-e FLASH-e VINE BIT-e

569. A bottle of mineral water.   *Eine Flasche, Mineralwasser.*
    EIN-e FLASH-e MIN-e-rahl-VASS-ah-BIT-e

570. Some lemonade.   *Etwas Limonade.*   **ET-vas lim-on-ADE**

571. Fruit juice.   *Fruchtsaft.*   **FRUSCHT-zaft**

572. Cider.   *Apfelwein.*   **AP-fel-vine**

573. A glass of milk.   *Ein Glass Milch.*   **EIN GLAHS MILSCH**

574. Tea with milk.   *Tee mit Milch.*   **TAY MIT MILSCH**

575. A bottle of red wine.   *Eine Flasche Rotwein.*
    EIN-e FLASH-e ROHT-vine

576. A glass of rosé.   *Ein Glas Rosé.*   **ein GLAHS row-ZAY**

577. A carafe of white wine.   *Eine Karaffe Weißwein.*
    EIN-e ka-RAFF-e VISE-vine

578. A beer.   *Ein Bier.*   **ein BEE-ah**

579. What draft beers do you have?
    Was für Faßbier haben Sie?
    vas fewr FASS-bee-ah HA-ben zee

580. I would like to have _____.
    Ich glaube ich nehme _____.
    isch GLAU-be isch NAY-meh

    _____ a local beer.   _____ *ein einheimisches Bier.*
        ein EIN-HIME-ish-es BEE-ah

    _____ a stout beer.   _____ *ein Dunkles.*
        ein DOONK-les BEE-ah

    _____ a lager.   _____ *ein Helles.*   **ein HELL-es**

    _____ a brown ale.   _____ *ein Starkbier.*
        ein SHTAHK BEE-ah

    _____ a Pilsener.   _____ *ein Pils.*   **ein PILS**

_____ a wheat beer.   _____ *ein Weißbier.*
ein VISE-BEE-ah

581. What's the house cocktail?
Was für ein Hausgetränk haben Sie?
vas FEWR ein HAUS-ge-TRAENK HA-ben zee?

582. A whiskey.   *Einen Whisky.*   **EIN-en VISS-kee**

583. An aperitif.   *Einen Aperitif.*   **EIN-en a-pair-i-TEEF**

584. An after-dinner drink.   *Ein Digestif.*   **ein dee-jest-eef**

Chapter 4
Socializing and Leisure

HOUSES OF WORSHIP

585. I am _____.   *Ich bin _____.*   **ISCH-bin**

_____ religious.   _____ *religiös.*   **RE-lee-ghee-OES**

_____ agnostic.   _____ *agnostisch.*   **ag-NOH-stisch**

_____ Christian.   _____ *christlich.*   **KRIST-lisch**

_____ Catholic.   _____ *katholish.*   **KAT-OH-lisch**

_____ Jewish.   _____ *jüdisch.*   **YEW-disch**

_____ Muslim.   _____ *moslemisch.*
mohz-LAY-misch

_____ an Atheist.   _____ *Atheist.*   **AH-tay-IST**

586. Is there _____ nearby?
Gibt es hier in der Nähe _____?
GIPT ess here in dair NAY-e

_____ a Protestant church.
_____ *eine protestantische Kirche.*
EIN-e prow-tes-TANT-isch-e KIR-sheh

_____ a Catholic church.
_____ *eine katholische Kirche.*
EIN-e kat-OWL-isch-e KIR-sche

_____ a synagogue.   _____ *eine Synagoge.*
EIN-e ZIN-a-GOH-ge

_____ a mosque.   _____ *eine Moschee.*
EIN-e mow-SHAY

_____ a religious site.   _____ *eine religiöse Stätte.*
EIN-e re-li-ghee-OEZ-e SHTAETT-e

When is the service?   *Wann ist der Gottesdienst?*
VANN ist dair GOTT-ess-DEENST

587.   Am I allowed to go inside?   *Darf ich eintreten?*
DARF isch EIN-tray-tn

FRIENDS AND SOCIAL NETWORKING

588.   Where is a good place to have a beer/a coffee/a coke?
Wo kann man hier ein Bier/einen Kaffee/eine Cola trinken?
**VOH KANN mann HEAH ein BEEAH/EIN-en KAFF-aye/
EIN-e KO-lah TRIN-ken**

589.   May I take you out for a coffee/a cola/a beer/ice cream?
*Darf ich Sie auf einen Kaffee/eine Cola/ ein Bier/ein Eis
einladen? (formal, singular or plural)*
**DARF isch ZEE auf EIN-en KAFF-aye/ EIN-e CO-lah/ EIN
BEEAH/EIN EIS EIN-lah-den**

*Darf ich dich auf einen Kaffee/eine Cola/ ein Bier/ein Eis
einladen? (informal, singular)*
**DARF isch DISCH auf-EIN-en KAFF-aye-/EIN-e CO-lah/EIN
BEEAH/EIN ICE EIN-lah-den**

590.   What do you like to do in your free time?
*Was machen Sie gern in Ihrer Freizeit? (formal, singular or
plural)*
VASS MAKH-en ZEE geahn in EE-rah FRY-tsite

Was machst du gern in deiner Freizeit? (informal, singular)
VASS MAKHST DOO geahn in DYE-nah FRY-tsite

591.   You look gorgeous!
Sie sehen umwerfend aus! (formal, singular or plural)
ZEE zay-en OOM-vair-fent-AUS

Du siehst umwerfend aus! (informal, singular)
DOO ZEEST OOM-vair-fent AUS

592.   You are really sweet!
Sie sind echt süß! (formal, singular or plural)
ZEE ZINT ESCHT ZEWS

Du bist echt süß! (informal, singular)
DOO BIST ESCHT ZEWS

593. I like you very much.
Ich habe Sie sehr gern. (formal, singular or plural)
ISCH HA-be zee ZAIR geahn

Ich habe dich sehr gern. (informal, singular)
ISCH HA-be disch ZAIR geahn

594. I find you very attractive.
Ich finde Sie sehr attraktiv. (formal, singular or plural)
ISCH FIN-de ZEE ZAIR AT-rak-TEEF

Ich finde dich sehr attraktiv. (informal, singular)
ISCH FIN-de DISCH ZAIR AT-rak-TEEF

595. May I have your _____?
Darf ich Ihre _____ haben? (formal, singular or plural)
DARF isch EE-re _____ HA-ben

Darf ich deine _____ haben? (formal, singular)
DARF isch DIE-ne _____ HA-ben

_____ phone number.   _____ *Telefonnummer.*
te-le-FOHN-NOOM-ah

_____ cell phone number.   _____ *Handynummer.*
HAN-dee-NOOM-ah

_____ e-mail address.   _____ *Email-Adresse.*
EE-male a-DRESS-e

_____ twitter address.   _____ *Twitteradresse.*
TVITT-e a-DRESS-e

596. Let's go dancing, shall we?   *Wie wär's mit tanzen?*
VEE VAIRS mit TAN-tsen

597. Can I see you again?
Kann ich Sie wiedersehen? (formal, singular or plural)
KANN isch zee VEE-da-ZAY-en

Kann ich dich wiedersehen? (informal)
KANN isch disch VEE-da-ZAY-en

SIGHTSEEING

Most German towns have a local Fremdenverkehrsamt (tourist office) that is an excellent resource for travelers. Don't hesitate to pay a visit. The staff is usually eager to suggest local attractions, recommend interesting excursions, and provide you with helpful maps, brochures and other useful information that will help you make the most of your time there.

598. Where is the nearest tourist office?
      Wo ist das hiesige Fremdenverkehrsamt?
      VOH ist dass HEE-zee-ge FREM-den-fa-KAIRS-AMT

599. What local attractions do you recommend?
      Was für Touristenattraktionen haben Sie?
      vass fewr tou-RIST-en-at-rak-tsee-OWN-en HA-ben zee

600. We're interested in a guided visit.
      Wir sind an einer Führung interessiert.
      VEE-ah ZINT an-EIN-ah FEWR-oong IN-te-ress-EERT

601. What are the hours of operation?
      Was sind die Öffnungszeiten?
      VAS ZINT dee OEFF-noongs-TSITE-en

602. How much is the entrance fee?
      Wieviel kostet der Eintritt?
      VEE-feel KOST-et dair EIN-tritt

603. Where can I buy tickets?
      Wo kann ich Eintrittskarten kaufen?
      VOH KANN isch EIN-tritts-kar-ten KAUF-en

604. I'd like two tickets for tonight's show.
      Ich möchte zwei Karten für die Aufführung heute Abend.
      isch MEWSH-te TSVEYE KAH-ten fewr dee AUF-fewr-oong
      HOY-te AH-bent

605. What time does it start/end?   *Wann beginnt/endet sie?*
      VANN be-GINNT/EN-det zee

606. Is there a reduced ticket price for _____.
      Gibt es verbilligte Karten für _____.
      GIPT ess fe-BILL-ig-te KAH-ten FEWR

      _____ seniors?   _____ *Senioren?*   **ze-nee-OW-ren**

      _____ students?   _____ *Schüler und Studenten?*
      SHEW-lah oont shtoo-DENT-en

      _____ children?   _____ *Kinder?*   **KIN-da**

_____ the unemployed?   _____ *Arbeitslose?*
AR-bites-LOH-ze

_____ groups?   _____ *Gruppen?*   **GROOP-en**

607. We'd like to visit _____.
Wir möchten _____ besuchen.
VEE-ah MEWSH-ten _____ be-SOOKH-en

_____ an art museum.
_____ *ein Kunstmuseum _____.*
ein KOONST-moo-ZAY-oom

_____ a cemetery.   _____ *einen Friedhof _____.*
EIN-en FREED-hohf

_____ the historic district.
_____ *die Altstadt _____.*
dee ALT-shtaht

_____ the church.   _____ *die Kirche _____.*
dee KIR-sche

_____ the castle.   _____ *das Schloss _____.*
dass SHLOSS

_____ a concert.   _____ *ein Konzert.*
ein kon-TSERT

_____ a play.   _____ *ein Theaterstück.*
ein tay-AH-tah-shtook

_____ a movie.   _____ *einen Film.*   **EIN-en FILM**

_____ an art exhibit.   _____ *eine Kunstausstellung*
EIN-e KOONST-aus-SHTELL-oong

_____ an opera.   _____ *eine Oper _____.*
EIN-e OH-pah

608. We'd like to go _____.   *Wir möchten _____ gehen.*
VEE-ah MEWHS-ten _____-GAY-en

_____ to a nightclub.
_____ *in einen Nachtclub _____.*
in EIN-en NAKHT-kloob

_____ to a bar.   _____ *in eine Bar _____.*
in EIN-e BAHR

_____ to a cinema.   _____ *ins Kino _____.*
ins KEE-noh

609. My kids and I would like to go _____.
Meine Kinder und ich möchten _____ gehen.
MINE-e KIN-da oont ISCH MEWSH-ten _____ GAY-en

_____ to the zoo.   _____ *in den Zoo* _____.
IN dayn TSOH

_____ to a playground.
_____ *auf den Spielplatz* _____.
AUF dayn SHPEEL-plats

_____ to a garden.   _____ *in einen Garten* _____.
in EIN-en GAR-ten

_____ to a pool.
_____ *in ein Schwimmbad* _____.
in EIN SHWIMM-bahd

610. Would it be possible _____.
Können wir _____ gehen?
KOENN-en VEE-ah _____ GAY-en

_____ to go a beach?   _____ *an den Strand* _____?
an dayn SHTRAHNT

_____ go to a park?   _____ *in den Park* _____?
IN dayn PAHK

_____ go to a botanical garden?
_____ *in den botanischen Garten* _____?
in dayn baw-TAHN-isch-en GAR-ten

_____ visit a cathedral?
_____ *in eine Kathedrale* _____?
in EIN-e KAT-ay-DRAH-leh

_____ to a football game?
_____ *zu einem Fußballspiel* _____.
tsoo EIN-em FOOS-ball-shpeel

HOBBIES

611. I'm interested in_____.
Ich interessiere mich für_____.
isch IN-tehr-ess-EE-re misch fewr

_____ movies.   _____ *Filme.*   FIL-meh
_____ architecture.   _____ *Architektur.*
AR-kee-tek-TOOR

_____ modern art.   _____ *moderne Kunst.*
moh-DAIRN-eh KOONST

612. I enjoy talking about _____.
Ich spreche gern über _____.
isch SHPRESCH-e GEAHN ew-beh

_____ religion.   _____ *Religion.*   **REH-lee-ghee-AWN**

_____ current events.   _____ *aktuelle Ereignisse.*
AK-too-ell-eh err-EIG-niss-e

_____ economics.   _____ *die Wirtschaft.*
dee VIRT-shaft

_____ science.   _____ *die Wissenschaften.*
dee VISS-en-shaft-en

613. Are you interested in politics?
Sind Sie an Politik interessiert? (formal, singular or plural)
ZINT-zee-an-POH-li-TEEK-IN-te-ress-eert

Seid ihr an Politik interessiert? (informal, plural)
ZITE EE-ah an POH-li-TEEK IN-te-ress-eert

Bist du an Politik interessiert? (informal, singular)
BIST doo an POH-li-TEEK IN-te-ress-eert

614. I agree.   *Stimmt.*   **SHTIMMT**

615. I totally disagree!   *Ganz und gar nicht!*
GAHNTS oont GAHR nischt

616. I'm studying _____.   *Ich studiere_____.*
ISCH shtoo-DEE-reh

_____ painting.   _____ *Malerei.*   **MAHL-e-RYE**

_____ music.   _____ *Musik.*   **moo-ZEEK**

_____ fashion.   _____ *Mode.*   **MOH-de**

_____ photography.   _____ *Fotografie.*
FOH-toh-gra-FEE

617. I really like_____.   *Ich finde _____ toll.*
isch FIN-de _____ TOHLL

_____ sports.   _____ *Sport _____.*   **SHPORT**

_____ reading.   _____ *Lesen _____.*   **LAY-zen**

_____ knitting.   _____ *Stricken* _____.
SHTRICK-en

_____ drawing.   _____ *Zeichnen* _____.
TSEISCH-nen

_____ sculpture.   _____ *Skulpturen*.
skoolp-TOOR-en

SPORTS

618.   Is there a place nearby where I can_____?
Wo kann man hier _____?
VOH kann man HEE-ah

_____ ski?   _____ *skilaufen?*   **SHEE-lau-fen**

_____ play tennis?   _____ *Tennis spielen?*
TEN-is SHPEE-len

_____ swim?   _____ *schwimmen?*   **SHWIM-an**

_____ go hiking?   _____ *wandern?*   **VAN-dern**

_____ go camping?   _____ *zelten?*   **TSEL-ten**

_____ mountain climb?   _____ *bergsteigen?*
BERG-shteig-en

_____ go biking?   _____ *radfahren?*
RAHT-faH-ren

_____ water ski?   _____ *Wasserski fahren?*
VAS-er-shee FAH-ren

_____ play golf?   _____ *Golf spielen?*
GOLLF SHPEEL-en

_____ go ice skating?   _____ *eislaufen?*
ICE-lauff-en

Chapter 5
Shopping

BANKING AND MONEY

619. Is there _____ nearby?
Gibt es hier in der Nähe _____?
GIPT ess HEE-ah in dair NAY-e

620. _____ A bank. _____ *Eine Bank.* **EIN-e BAHNK**

621. _____ An ATM. _____ *einen Geldautomaten.*
EIN-en GELT-au-toh-MA-ten

622. _____ An American Express office.
_____ *Ein American Express Büro.*
EIN ah-MER-i-cahn ex-PRESS BEW-roh

623. _____ A currency exchange.
_____ *Eine Geldwechselstube.*
EIN-e GELT-VEX-l-SHTOO-be

624. I'd like _____. *Ich möchte _____.* **isch MEWSH-te**
_____ change some money. _____ *Geld wechseln.*
GELT VEX-ln

_____ cash a traveler's check.
_____ *einen Travelerscheck einlösen.*
EIN-en TRAV-e-lah SHECK EIN-lews-en

_____ withdraw some money. _____ *Geld abheben.*
GELT AP-hay-ben

625.   May I please have _____?
       Kann ich bitte _____ haben?
       KANN isch BIT-e _____ HA-ben

       _____ some change?   _____ *Wechselgeld* _____?
              VEX-l-GELT

       _____ smaller bills?
       _____ *kleinere Scheine* _____?
              KLEIN-e-re SHINE-e

626.   He wrote a bad check.
       Er hat einen ungedeckten Scheck ausgestellt.
       AIR hat EIN-en OON-ge-DECK-ten SHECK AUS-ge-shtellt

SHOPPING

627.   I'd like to do a bit of window shopping.
       Ich möchte einen Schaufensterbummel machen.
       isch MEWSH-te EIN-en SHAU-fens-tah-BUMM-el MAKH-en

628.   How much does this cost?   *Wieviel kostet das?*
       VEE-FEEL KOS-tet dass

629.   Where are the cash registers, please?
       Wo geht's bitte zu den Kassen?
       VOH GAITS BIT-e tsoo dain CASS-en?

630.   I'd like to pay_____.
       Ich möchte _____ zahlen.
       isch MEWSH-te _____ TSAH-len

       _____ with cash.   _____ *bar* _____.   **BAHR**
       _____ by check.   _____ *per Scheck* _____.
              pair SHECK

       _____ by credit card.
       _____ *per Kreditkarte* _____.
              pair cray-DEET kar-te

631.   May I have the receipt?
       Kann ich bitte die Quittung haben?
       KANN isch BIT-e dee KVIT-oong HA-ben

SHOPPING 75

632. Is there a(n) _____ nearby?
Gibt es hier in der Nähe _____?
GIPT ess HEE-ah in dair NAY-e?

_____ A department store.   _____ *Ein Kaufhaus.*
ein KAUF-house

_____ A clothing store.
_____ *Ein Bekleidungsgeschäft.*
EIN be-KLIDE-oongs-ge-SHEFT

_____ A boutique.   _____ *Eine Boutique.*
EIN-e boo-TEEK

_____ A shoe store.   _____ *Ein Schuhgeschäft.*
ein SHOO-ge-SHEFT

_____ A stationer's.   _____ *Ein Papierwarengeschäft.*
ein pah-PEER-vah-ren-ge-SHEFT

_____ A bookstore.   _____ *Eine Buchhandlung.*
EIN-e BOOKH-HAND-loong

_____ A jewelry store.   _____ *Einen Juwelenladen.*
EIN-en you-VE-len-LAH-den

_____ A tobacconist.   _____ *Einen Tabakladen.*
EIN-en ta-BAK-LAH-den

_____ A bakery.   _____ *Eine Bäckerei.*
EIN-e beck-ah-RYE

_____ A pastry shop.   _____ *Eine Konditorei.*
EIN-e KON-di-taw-RYE

_____ A convenience store.
_____ *Ein 24-Stunden-Geschäft.*
EIN FEER-oont-tswahn-tsisch-SHTOON-den ge-SHEFT

_____ A supermarket.   _____ *Einen Supermarkt.*
EIN-en ZOO-pah-MARKT

_____ A deli.   _____ *Einen Delikatessenladen.*
EIN-en de-lee-kah-TESS-en-LAH-den

_____ A health-food store.   _____ *Ein Reformhaus.*
ein re-FORM-house

_____ An open-air market.
_____ *Einen Markt unter freiem Himmel.*
EIN-en MARKT oon-tah FRY-em HIMM-l

_____ A flower shop. _____ *Einen Blumenladen.*
EIN-en BLOOM-en-LAH-den

_____ A flea market. _____ *Einen Flohmarkt.*
EIN-en FLOH-markt

_____ A dry cleaning store.
_____ *Eine chemische Reinigung.*
EIN-e KHE-misch-e RYE-nee-goong

_____ A laundromat. _____ *Einen Waschsalon.*
EIN-en VASH-zah-lawn

_____ A camera store. _____ *Ein Photogeschäft.*
EIN FOH-toh-ge-SHEFT

_____ A newsstand. _____ *Ein Zeitungskiosk.*
EIN TSITE-oongs-KEE-osk

_____ A hair salon. _____ *Einen Friseursalon.*
EIN-en free-ZEWR-zah-LAWN

_____ A beauty salon. _____ *Einen Schönheitssalon.*
EIN-en SHEWN-hites-zah-LAWN

_____ A hardware store.
_____ *Einen Eisenwarenladen.*
EIN-en IZE-en-vah-ren-LAH-den

633. At the Department Store. *Im Kaufhaus.* im KAUF-house

634. Where is the _____ department?
Wo finde ich die _____ abteilung?
VOH FIN-de isch dee _____ AP-teil-oong

_____ ladies' clothing _____.
_____ *Damenbekleidungs _____.*
DAH-men-be-KLIDE-oongs

_____ gentlemen's clothing_____.
_____ *Herrenbekleidungs_____.*
HAIR-en-be-KLIDE-oongs

_____ children's clothing_____.
_____ *Kinderbekleidungs_____.*
KIN-dah-be-KLIDE-oongs

_____ shoe _____. _____ *Schuhwaren _____.*
SHOO-vah-ren

_____ housewares _____.
_____ *Haushaltswaren* _____.
HAUS-halts-VAH-ren

_____ electronics _____.
_____ *Elektronikwaren* _____.
ELL-eck-TRAWN-eeck-vah-ren

_____ toys _____.   _____ *Spielwaren* _____.
SHPEEL-vah-ren

_____ cosmetics _____.   _____ *Kosmetik* _____.
koz-may-tik

635. At the Clothing Store/Boutique.
Im Bekleidungswarengeschäft/in der Boutique.
im be-KLIDE-oongs-vah-ren-ge-SHEFT/IN dair boo-TEEK

636. I'm looking for something _____.
Ich suche etwas _____.
isch SOO-khe ET-vas

_____ bigger.   _____ *Größeres.*   **GREW-se-res**
_____ smaller.   _____ *Kleineres.*   **KLINE-e-res**
_____ less expensive.   _____ *Preiswerteres.*
PREIS-vair-tah-res

637. Do you have anything else?   *Haben Sie etwas Anderes?*
HA-ben zee ET-vas AN-de-res?

638. May I try this on?   *Kann ich das anprobieren?*
KANN isch dass AN-proh-BEER-en

639. Do you want a different one?
Möchten Sie ein anderes Stück?
MEWSH-ten zee ein AN-de-res SHTEWK?

640. Where is the changing room?   *Wo ist der Umkleideraum?*
VOH ist dair OOM-klide-e-raum

641. Where can I buy _____?   *Wo kann ich* _____ *kaufen?*
VOH kann isch _____ KAUF-en

_____ A dress.   _____ *Ein Kleid* _____.   **ein KLITE**
_____ A skirt.   _____ *Einen Rock* _____.
EIN-en ROK

_____ Some pants.   _____ *Eine Hose* _____.
EIN-e HOH-ze

_____ A shirt.   _____ *Ein Hemd* _____.
ein HEMT

_____ A dress shirt.   _____ *Ein Frackhemd* _____.
ein FRAK-hemt

_____ An undershirt.   _____ *Ein Unterhemd* _____.
EIN OON-tah-hemt

_____ Underpants.   _____ *Eine Unterhose* _____.
EIN-e OON-tah-HOH-ze

_____ A slip.   _____ *Einen Unterrock* _____.
EIN-en OON-tah-rok

_____ A bra.   _____ *Einen BH* _____.
EIN-en BAY-HAH

_____ A tie.   _____ *Eine Krawatte* _____.
EIN-e krah-VAT-te

_____ pajamas.   _____ *Einen Schlafanzug* _____.
EIN-en SHLAHF-AN-tsook

_____ A nightgown.   _____ *Ein Nachthemd* _____.
EIN NAKHT-hemt

_____ gloves.   _____ *Handschuhe* _____.
HANT-shoo-e

_____ A winter hatv.
_____ *Eine Wintermütze* _____.
EIN-e VIN-tah-MEWT-zeh

_____ A winter coat (long).
_____ *Ein Wintermantel* _____.
EIN VIN-tah-MANN-tl

_____ A winter coat (short).
_____ *Eine Winterjacke* _____.
EIN-e VIN-tah-YAHK-e

_____ A raincoat.   _____ *Ein Regenmantel* _____.
EIN RAY-gen-MAN-tl

_____ socks _____.   _____ *Socken* _____.
ZOK-en

_____ stockings _____.   _____ *Kniestrümpfe* _____.
KNEE-shtrewmp-fe

_____ Some tights _____.
_____ *Eine Strumpfhose* _____.
EIN-e SHTROOMPF-hoh-ze

_____ A scarf.   _____ *Einen Schal* _____.
EIN-en SHAHL

_____ A sweater.   _____ *Einen Pullover* _____.
EIN-en PULL-OVER

_____ A turtleneck sweater.
_____ *Einen Rollkragenpullover* _____.
EIN-en ROLL-krah-gen-PULL-OVER

_____ A blouse.   _____ *Eine Bluse* _____.
EIN-e BLOO-ze

_____ A tank top.
_____ *Ein Trägerhemdchen* _____.
ein TRAY-gah-HEMT-schyen

_____ A swimsuit.   _____ *Einen Badeanzug* _____.
EIN-en BAH-de-AN-tsook

_____ Swimtrunks.   _____ *Eine Badehose* _____.
EIN-e BAH-de-HOH-ze

_____ A sunhat.   _____ *Einen Sonnenhut* _____.
EIN-en ZONN-en-HOOT

_____ Sunglasses.   _____ *Eine Sonnenbrille* _____.
EIN-e ZONN-en-BRILL-e

_____ Sunscreen.   _____ *Sonnenschutzcreme* _____.
ZONN-en-SHUHTS-craym-e

_____ A beach towel.   _____ *Ein Badetuch* _____.
EIN BAH-de-TOOKH

_____ A beach bag.   _____ *Eine Badetasche* _____.
EIN-e BAH-de-TASH-e

_____ A purse.   _____ *Eine Handtasche* _____.
EIN-e HANT-TASH-e

642. At the Shoe Store.   *Im Schuhgeschäft.*
Im SHOO-ge-SHEFT

643. What shoe size do you wear?   *Welche Schuhgröße tragen Sie*
VEL-she SHOO-grews-e TRAH-gen ZEE

644. I wear size _____.   *Ich trage Größe* _____.
isch TRAH-ge GREWS-e

645. I'm looking _____.   *Ich suche _____.*
     isch ZOO-khe

     _____ sandals.   _____ *Sandalen.*   **zan-DAH-len**

     _____ sneakers.   _____ *Turnschuhe.*
     TOORN-shoo-e

     _____ high heels.   _____ *hockhackige Schuhe.*
     HOHKH-hack-ee-ge SHOOh-e

     _____ flip flops.   _____ *Badelatschen.*
     BAH-de-LAH-tschen

     _____ Tennis shoes.   _____ *Tennisschuhe.*
     TEN-is-SHOO-e

     _____ hiking boots.   _____ *Wanderstiefel.*
     VAN-dah-SHTEE-fl

     _____ winter boots.   _____ *Winterstiefel.*
     VIN-tah-SHTEE-fl.

     _____ Some rubber boots.   _____ *Gummistiefel.*
     GOOM-ee-SHTEE-fl

646. At the Bookstore.   *In der Buchhandlung.*
     IN dair BOOKH-hand-loong

647. I'm looking for a _____.   *Ich suche _____.*
     isch ZOO-khe

     _____ a book.   _____ *ein Buch.*   **ein BOOKH**

     _____ something in English.
     _____ *etwas auf Englisch.*
     ET-vass auf ENG-lisch

     _____ a novel.   _____ *einen Roman.*
     EIN-en roh-MAHN

     _____ a guide book.   _____ *einen Touristenführer.*
     EIN-en tou-RIST-en-FEW-rah

     _____ an English-German dictionary.
     _____ *ein englisch-deutsches Wörterbuch.*
     ein ENG-lisch-DOITSH-es VOER-tah-bookh

     _____ a children's book.   _____ *ein Kinderbuch.*
     ein KIN-dah-bookh

     _____ an audiobook.   _____ *ein Hörbuch.*
     EIN HOER-bookh

_____ a reading lamp.   _____ *eine Leselampe.*
   EIN-e LAY-ze-LAM-pe

_____ a graphic novel.   _____ *einen Comicroman.*
   EIN-en KOM-ik-roh-MAHN

_____ an eBook reader.
_____ *ein elektronisches Lesegerät.*
   EIN EH-lek-TRAWN-ish-es LAY-ze-ge-rait

648. At the Stationery Store.   *In der Schreibwarenhandlung.*
   IN dair SHRIBE-vah-ren-HANT-loong

649. I'd like to buy _____.   *Ich möchte _____ kaufen.*
   isch MEWSH-te _____ KAUF-en

_____ a pen.   _____ *einen Kugelschreiber _____.*
   EIN-en KOO-gl-SHRY-beh

_____ a pencil.   _____ *einen Bleistift _____.*
   EIN-en BLY-shtift

_____ a pad of paper.
_____ *einen Notizblock _____.*
   EIN-en noh-TEETS-blohck

_____ some envelopes.   _____ *Briefumschläge.*
   BREEF-OOM-shlay-ge

650. At the Jewelry Store.   *Im Juwelierladen.*
   IM YEW-ve-LEER-lah-den

651. I'd like to have this watch repaired.
   Ich möchte diese Uhr reparieren lassen.
   isch MEWSH-te DEE-ze Ooah re-pah-REER-en LASS-en

652. Do you have a battery for this watch?
   Haben Sie eine Batterie für diese Uhr?
   HA-ben zee EIN-e BATT-e-REE fewr DEE-ze OOah

653. I'd like to buy _____.   *Ich möchte _____ kaufen.*
   isch MEWSH-te _____ KAUF-en

_____ a present.   _____ *ein Geschenk _____.*
   ein ge-SHENK

_____ a bracelet.   _____ *ein Armband _____.*
   ein ARM-bant

_____ an anklet.   _____ *ein Fußkettchen* _____.
ein FOOS-kett-shen

_____ a pin.   _____ *eine Brosche* _____.
EIN-e BROH-sheh

_____ a ring.   _____ *einen Ring* _____.
EIN-en RING

_____ earrings.   _____ *Ohrringe* _____.
OHR-ing-e

_____ a necklace.   _____ *eine Halskette* _____.
EIN-e HALS-kett-e

654. At the Tobacco Shop.   *Im Tabakladen.*   **im TA-back-LA-den**

655. A pack of cigarettes, please.
Eine Schachtel Zigaretten, bitte.
EIN-e SHAKH-tl TSI-gah-RETT-en BIT-e

656. A pack of pipe tobacco, please.
Eine Packung Pfeifentabak, bitte.
EIN-e PACK-oong PFIFE-en-tah-BACK BIT-e

657. A lighter.   *Ein Feuerzeug.*   **EIN FOY-ah-TSOIK**

658. Matches.   *Streichhölzer.*   **SHTRYSH-hohl-tseh**

659. Some stamps.   *Briefmarken.*   **BREEF-mar-ken**

660. At the Bakery.   *Beim Bäcker.*   **bime BECK-ah**

661. I'd like _____.   *Ich möchte* _____.   **isch-MEWSH-te**

_____ a loaf of bread.   _____ *einen Laib Brot.*
EIN-en LEIP BROHT

_____ a half a loaf of bread.
_____ *einen halben Laib Brot.*
EIN-en HAL-ben leip BROHT

_____ some rolls.   _____ *Brötchen.*   **BROET-shee-en**

_____ whole wheat bread.   _____ *Vollkornbrot.*
FAWL-korn-BROHT

_____ rye bread.   _____ *Roggenbrot.*
ROG-en-BROHT

_____ sunflower seed bread.   _____ *Sonnenblumenbrot.*
ZON-en-BLOOM-en-BROHT

_____ pumpernickel bread.   _____ *Pumpernickelbrot.*
POOMP-ah-NICK-l-BROHT

662. At the Pastry Shop.   *Beim Konditor.*   **byme kon-DEE-towr**

663. We'd like _____.   *Wir möchten _____.*
VEE-ah MEWSH-ten

_____ two croissants.   _____ *zwei Hörnchen.*
TSVEYE HERN-shyen

_____ a chocolate croissant.
_____ *ein Schokoladencroissant.*
EIN SHAW-koh-LAH-den-CWA-sahnt

_____ a raisin bun.   _____ *eine Rosinenschnecke.*
EIN-e roh-ZEEN-en-SHNECK-e

_____ some pastries.   _____ *Gebäck.*   **ge-BECK**

_____ some cookies.   _____ *Plätzchen.*
PLETS-shyen

664. At the Supermarket.   *Im Supermarkt.*
im ZOO-pah-MARKT

665. Where is the _____ section?
Wo ist die _____ Abteilung?
VOH ist dee-_____ AP-tile-oong

_____ Cheese.   _____ *Käse _____.*   **KAY-zeh**

_____ Wine and spirits.
_____ *Wein und Spirituousen _____.*
VINE oont SPEE-REE-too-OH-zen

_____ Candy.   _____ *Süßwaren _____.*
SUES-vah-ren

_____ Meat and Cold Cuts.
_____ *Fleisch und Wurst.*
FLYSH oont VOORSHT

_____ Fish and poultry.
_____ *Fisch und Geflügel _____.*
FISH oont ge-FLEW-gl

_____ Dairy products.   _____ *Milchprodukte.*
MILSCH-proh-DOOK-te

666. At the Deli.   *Im Delikatessenladen.*
      IM de-lee-kah-TESS-en-LAH-den

667. Do you have take-out?
      Haben Sie Gerichte zum Mitnehmen?
      HA-ben zee ge-RISH-te tsoom MIT-nay-men?

668. At the Flower Shop.   *Beim Floristen.*   **byme floh-RISS-ten**

669. Do you like flowers?

      Mögen Sie Blumen? (formal, singular or plural)
      MEW-gen ZEE BLOOM-en

      Mögt ihr Blumen? (informal, plural)
      MOEGT EE-ah BLOOM-en

      Magst du Blumen? (informal, singular)
      MAHGST DOO BLOOM-en

670. I'd like to buy a bouquet of flowers.
      Ich möchte einen Blumenstrauß kaufen.
      isch MEWSH-te EIN-en BLOOM-en-shtrowss KAUF-en

671. You can choose them.   *Sie können auswählen.*
      ZEE KOENN-en AUS-vay-len

672. I'd like a combination of flowers.
      Stellen Sie mir einen Strauß zusammen.
      SHTELL-en zee meer EIN-en SHTROWSS tsoo-ZAM-en

673. I would like _____.   *Ich möchte _____.*
      isch MEWSH-te

      _____ roses.   _____ *Rosen.*   **ROHZ-en**

      _____ tulips.   _____ *Tulpen.*   **TOOL-pen**

      _____ some daisies.   _____ *Margariten.*
      MAR-ga-REET-en

      _____ peonies.   _____ *Pfingstrosen.*
      PFINGST-roh-zen

674. Will I need to change the water daily?
      Muss ich das Wasser täglich wechseln?
      MOUSSE isch dass VASS-ah TAYG-lisch VEX-ln

675. Can you wrap the bouquet in paper?
Können Sie den Strauß in Papier einwickeln?
KOENN-en zee dain shtrowss in pah-PEE-ah EIN-vick-ln

676. I'd like to send some flowers to _____.
Ich möchte Blumen _____ schicken.
isch MEWSH-te BLOOM-en _____ SHICK-en

_____ this address.   _____ *an diese Adresse* _____.
an DEE-ze a-DRESS-e

_____ this person.   _____ *zu dieser Person* _____.
tsoo DEE-zah PAIR-ZOHN

677. I'd like a house plant.   *Ich möchte eine Zimmerpflanze.*
isch MEWSH-te EIN-e TSIM-ah-PFLANTS-e

678. Do you sell potted flowers?   *Verkaufen Sie Topfblumen?*
fer-KAUF-en zee TOPF-bloom-en

679. At the Dry Cleaners.   *In der Reinigung.*
in dair RINE-ee-goong

680. Do you have a laundry service?
Haben Sie einen Reinigungsdienst?
HA-ben zee EIN-en RINE-ee-goongs-deenst

681. When will my things be ready?
Wann sind meine Sachen fertig?
VANN zint MINE-e ZA-khen FER-tisch

682. Can you iron these?   *Können Sie das bügeln?*
KOENN-en zee DASS BEW-geln

683. Can you shorten these pants?
Können Sie diese Hose kürzen?
KOENN-en zee DEE-ze HO-ze KEWR-tsen?

684. Do you do mending?   *Machen Sie auch Reparaturen?*
MAKH-en zee AUKH re-pah-ra-TOOR-en?

685. At the Laundromat.   *Im Waschsalon.*   **im VASH-ZAH-lon**

686. What coins do I need for these machines?
Was für Münzen brauche ich für diese Maschinen?
VASS fewr MUEN-tsen BRAU-khe isch fewr dee-ze MAH-SHEE-nen

687. Where can I buy some detergent?
Wo kann ich Waschmittel kaufen?
VOH kann isch VASH-MIT-tl KAUF-en?

688. Is there any powder detergent?   *Gibt es hier Waschpulver?*
GIPT ess HEE-ah VASH-pul-fah?

689. Where can I dry my clothes?
Wo kann ich meine Wäsche trocknen?
VOH kann isch MINE-e VAY-sheh TRAWK-nen?

690. At the Camera Store.   *Im Photogeschäft.*
im FOH-toh-ge-SHAEFT

691. I'm looking for _____.   *Ich suche nach _____.*
ish ZOO-khe NAKH

_____ a digital camera.
_____ *einer digitalen Kamera.*
EIN-ah di-ghee-TAHL-en KAM-a-rah

_____ memory card for this camera.
_____ *einer Speicherkarte für diese Kamera.*
EIN-e SHPY-sha-KAR-te fewr DEE-ze KAM-a-rah

_____ batteries for my camera.
_____ *Batterien für meine Kamera.*
BAT-a-REE-en fewr MINE-e KAM-a-rah

_____ USB cable for my camera.
_____ *einem USB-Kabel für diese Kamera.*
EIN-em OO-ESS-BAY KAH-bl fewr DEE-ze KAM-a-rah

_____ adapter for this camera.
_____ *einem Adapter für diese Kamera.*
EIN-em a-DAHP-te fewr DEE-ze KAM-a-rah

692. Can you suggest _____?
Können Sie _____ empfehlen?
KOENN-en zee _____ emp-FAY-len

_____ a point-and-shoot camera.
_____ *eine Kompaktkamera _____.*
EIN-e KOMM-PAKT-KAM-a-rah

_____ a mid-range camera?
_____ *eine 35-mm-Kamera?*

EIN-e FUENF-oont-dry-sisch MIL-ee-may-tah
KAM-a-rah

_____ a dslr camera.
_____ *eine digitale Spiegelreflexkamera.*
EIN-e DI-gee-TAHL-e SHPEE-gl-re-FLEX-
KAM-a-rah

693. Can this be used abroad?
Kann ich das im Ausland benutzen?
KANN ISCH dass im AUS-lant be-NOOTS-en

694. Will I need a different plug/adapte?
Brauche ich einen anderen Stecker/Adapter?
BRAU-khe isch EIN-en AN-da-ren SHTECK-ah/a-DAP-tah

695. Can you show what lenses you carry?
Können Sie mir Ihre Lensen zeigen?
KOENN-nen zee meer EE-re LENZ-en TSIGE-en

696. Do you carry cleaning kits?   *Führen Sie Reinigungssets?*
FEWR-en zee RINE-ee-goongs-SETS

697. At the Newsstand.   *Am Zeitungsstand.*
AM TSITE-oongs-shtant

698. A newspaper, please.   *Eine Zeitung, bitte.*
EIN-e TSITE-oong BIT-e

699. Where are the English language magazines?
Wo sind die englischsprachigen Magazine?
VOH zint dee ENG-lish-SHPRAH-khee-gen MA-ga-TSEE-ne

700. At the Hair Salon.   *Beim Frisör.*   BYME free-ZEWR

701. I'd like to make an appointment.
Ich möchte einen Termin haben.
isch MEWSH-te EIN-en tair-MEEN HA-ben

702. Do you take walk-ins?   *Nehmen Sie auch Laufkundschaft?*
NAY-men ZEE aukh LAUF-koont-SHAHFT

703. I'd like _____.   *Ich möchte.*   isch MEWSH-te

_____ a cut.   _____ *einen Haarschnitt.*
EIN-en HAHR-shnitt

_____ a blow-out.   _____ *Waschen und Fönen.*
VASH-en oont FEWN-en

_____ high lights.   _____ *Strähnchen.*
STHRAYN-schyen

_____ the bangs trimmed.
_____ *den Pony schneiden lassen.*
dain POHN-ee SHNEYE-den LASS-en

MEASUREMENTS

704. 500 grams of _____.   *500 Gramm _____.*
FEWNF-hoon-dert GRAMM

705. A kilo of _____.   *Ein Kilo _____.*   **EIN KEE-low**

706. A half a kilo of _____.   *Ein halbes Kilo _____.*
EIN HAL-bes KEE-low

707. One pound of _____.   *Ein Pfund _____.*
EIN PFOONT

708. A bottle of _____.   *Eine Flasche _____.*
EIN-e FLAHSH-e

709. A liter of _____.   *Ein Liter _____.*   **EIN LEE-tah**

710. A glass of _____.   *Ein Glas _____.*   **ein GLAHS**

711. A slice of _____ (bread).   *Eine Scheibe _____.*
EIN-e SHY-be

712. A package of _____.   *Eine Packung _____.*
EIN-e PAHK-oong

713. A piece of _____.   *Ein Stück _____.*   **ein SHTOOK**

714. A little bit of _____.   *Ein bisschen _____.*
ein BISS-shyen

715. A box of _____.   *Eine Schachtel _____.*
EIN-e SHAKH-tl

716. A handful of _____.   *Eine Handvoll _____.*
EIN-e HANT-fawll

717. A can of _____.   *Eine Dose _____.*   **EIN-e DOH-ze**

718. A dozen _____.   *Ein Dutzend _____.*
ein DOOTS-ent

719. A jar of _____.   *Ein Glas _____.*   **ein GLAHS**

720. More _____.   *Noch etwas _____.*   **NOKH ET-vass**

721. Less _____.   *Nicht soviel _____.*   **NISCHT ZOH-feel**

722. That's enough.   *Das reicht.*   **dass REISCHT**

COLORS

723. Blue.   *Blau.*   **BLAU**

724. Green.   *Grün.*   **GREWN**

725. Red.   *Rot.*   **ROHT**

726. White.   *Weiß.*   **VISE**

727. Purple.   *Lila.*   **LEE-lah**

728. Black.   *Schwarz.*   **SHWARTS**

729. Brown.   *Braun.*   **BROWN**

730. Yellow.   *Gelb.*   **GELP**

731. Orange.   *Orange.*   **oh-RANTSH**

732. Pink.   *Rosav.*   **ROH-za**

733. Maybe another color?   *Wie wär's mit einer anderen Farbe?*
vee VAIRS mit EIN-ah AN-de-ren FAR-be

734. I love this color.   *Ich mag diese Farbe sehr.*
isch MAWG DEE-ze FAR-be ZAIR

735. Something darker?   *Etwas dunkler, vielleicht?*
ET-vass DOONK-lah fee-LEISCHT

736. Something lighter?   *Etwas heller, vielleicht?*
ET-vass HELL-ah fee-LEISCHT

737. Something striped?   *Etwas Gestreiftes, vielleicht?*
ET-vass ge-SHTRIFE-tes fee-LEISCHT

738. Something with polka dots?
Etwas Getupftes, vielleicht?
ET-vass ge-TOOPF-tes fee-LEISCHT

Chapter 6
Health

If you are feeling under the weather while traveling, make your first stop at the "Apotheke" (the pharmacy). A German pharmacy is quite different from its American counterpart, as it is possible in Germany to consult a pharmacist before contacting a physician. At the pharmacy, you'll be able to get advice, fill prescriptions, and buy over-the-counter medications. Unlike in the United States, these medications aren't available in supermarkets. If you need after-hours attention, look for a "Notapotheke" or a "Nachtapotheke," which must be open 24 hours according to German law. Regular pharmacies should have a sign posted that identifies the closest after-hours pharmacy. German pharmacies are easily recognized by the red letter "A" with a stylized snake and bowl.

AT THE PHARMACY

739. Where is the nearest pharmacy?
Wo ist die nächste Apotheke?
VOH ist dee NAYKHST-eh AP-oh-TAY-keh

740. Is there a 24-hour pharmacy nearby?
Gibt es hier in der Nähe eine Not/Nachtapotheke?
GIPT ess HEE-ah in dair NAY-eh EIN-e NOHT/NAKHT-AP-oh-TAY-keh

741. Do I need a prescription?   *Brauche ich ein Rezept?*
BRAU-khe ISCH ein re-TSEPT

742. I don't have a prescription.   *Ich habe kein Rezept.*
isch HA-be KINE re-TSEPT

743. My prescription is from an American doctor.
      Mein Rezept ist von einem US-Doktor ausgestellt.
      MINE re-TSEPT ist fawn EIN-em OO-ESS-DOK-tohr AUS-ge-SHTELLT

744. Do you have a sample of this?
      Haben Sie eine Kostprobe dafür?
      HA-ben ZEE EIN-e KOHST-proh-beh da-FEWR

745. Is this product appropriate for children?
      Ist das für Kinder geeignet?
      IST dass FEWR KIN-dah ge-EIG-net

746. What are the potential side-effects of this?
      Was sind mögliche Nebenwirkungen?
      VASS zint MEWG-lisch-e NAY-ben-VIRK-oong-en

747. I'd like to buy _____.   *Ich möchte _____ kaufen.*
      isch MEWSH-te _____ KAUF-en

      _____ aspirin.   _____ *Aspirin.*   **ASS-pee-REEN**

      _____ vitamins.   _____ *Vitamine.*
      VEE-tah-MEEN-e

      _____ bandages.   _____ *Pflaster.*   **PFLAS-tah**

      _____ Kleenex.   _____ *Papiertaschentücher.*
      pah-PEEah-TASH-en-TEW-schah

      _____ cough drops.   _____ *Hustenpastillen.*
      HOOST-ten-pas-TILL-en

748. I need some medication for _____.
      Ich brauche etwas gegen _____.
      isch BRAU-khe ET-vass GAY-gen

      _____ a headache.   _____ *Kopfschmerzen.*
      KOPF-shmair-tsen

      _____ pain.   _____ *Schmerzen.*   **SHMAIR-tsen**

      _____ a cold.   _____ *eine Erkältung.*
      EIN-e air-KELL-toong

      _____ the flu.   _____ *die Grippe.*   **dee GRIPP-e**

      _____ allergies.   _____ *Allergien.*   **ALL-air-GEE-en**

      _____ a cough.   _____ *Husten.*   **HOOS-ten**

_____ a bee sting.   _____ *einen Bienenstich.*
EIN-en BEE-nen-SHTISCH

_____ cramps.   _____ *Krämpfe.*   **KREM-pfeh**

749. I need _____.   *Ich brauche _____.*   **isch BRAU-khe**

_____ pills.   _____ *Tabletten.*   **tah-BLETT-en**

_____ a suppository.   _____ *ein Zäpfchen.*
EIN TSAEPF-schyen

AT THE DRUGSTORE

In Germany, you usually buy cosmetics and items related to personal hygiene at a "Drogeriemarkt," or simply "Drogerie." This establishment is reminiscent of an American drugstore chain, but it does not have prescription or non-prescription medications for sale.

750. Can you recommend _____?
Können Sie _____ empfehlen?
KOENN-en ZEE- _____ emp-FAY-len

_____ a good shampoo.
_____ *ein gutes Shampoo _____.*
EIN GOOT-es SHAM-poo

_____ good soap.
_____ *eine gute Seife _____.*
EIN-e GOOT-e ZIFE-e

751. What do you have in the way of _____?
Was für _____ haben Sie?
VASS fewr _____ HA-ben ZEE

_____ make-up?   _____ *Makeup _____?*
MAY-kup

_____ perfume?   _____ *Parfüm _____?*
par-FEWM

752. I need _____.   *Ich brauche _____.*   **isch BRAU-khe**

_____ a toothbrush.   _____ *eine Zahnbürste.*
EIN-e TSAHN-bewrs-te

_____ toothpaste.   _____ *Zahnpasta.*
TSAHN-PASS-tah

_____ some dental floss.   _____ *Zahnseide.*
TSAHN-zye-de

_____ some shaving cream.   _____ *Rasiercreme.*
ra-ZEER-cray-meh

753. Do you carry this brand of _____.
Haben Sie diese Sorte _____.
HA-ben zee DEE-ze ZAWR-te

_____ cleanser?   _____ *Reiniger?*   **RYE-nee-gah**

_____ razor?   _____ *Rasierer?*   **ra-ZEER-ah**

_____ a body lotion.   _____ *eine Körperlotion.*
EIN-e KEWR-peh-lowts-YOWN

_____ tampons.   _____ *Tampons.*   **TAM-pawns**

_____ feminine napkins.   _____ *Binden.*   **BIN-den**

_____ condoms.   _____ *Kondome.*   **con-DOW-meh**

754. What contact lens solution do you have?
Was für Marken an Kontaktlinsenlösung haben Sie?
**VASS fewr MAR-ken an kon-TAKT-lins-en-LEWS-oong
HA-ben zee**

755. What kind of diapers do you sell?
Was für Babywindeln führen Sie?
VASS fewr BAY-bee-VIN-deln FEWR-en ZEE

756. Do you sell baby wipes, too?
Führen Sie auch Babywischtücher?
FEWR-en ZEE owkh BAY-bee-VISH-tew-schah

757. Do you have baby bottles like this one?
Haben Sie solche Babytrinkflaschen?
HA-ben zee SAWL-sche BAY-bee-TRINK-flahsh-en

758. Please show me what you have in the way of sunscreen.
Bitte zeigen Sie mir ihre Sonnenschutzprodukte.
**BIT-e TSYG-en ZEE meer EE-re ZONN-en-SHOOTS-proh-
DOOK-te**

759. I'd like to buy a _____.   *Ich möchte _____ kaufen.*
isch MEWSH-te _____ KAUF-en

_____ a self-tanner.
_____ *eine Selbstbräunungscreme* _____.
EIN-e SELPST-BROY-noongs-CRAY-meh

_____ an after-sun cream.
_____ *etwas für nach dem Sonnenbaden.*
ET-vass fewr NAKH daim SONN-en-BAH-den

760. Do you have something with a stronger spf?
Haben Sie etwas mit einem größeren
Sonnenschutzfaktor?
HA-ben zee ET-vass mit EIN-em GROESS-e-ren ZONN-en-
SHOOTS-FAK-towr

761. Do you have something for a sunburn?
Haben Sie etwas gegen Sonnenbrand?
HA-ben zee ET-vass GAY-gen ZONN-en-BRAHNT

SEEING A DOCTOR

762. I am (very) sick.   *Ich fühle mich sehr krank.*
isch FEWL-e MISCH ZAIR krank

763. I need to be seen.
Ich brauche einen Arzt/eine Ärztin.
isch BRAU-khe EIN-en ARTST/EIN-e-AYRTS-tin

764. Where does it hurt?   *Wo tut's weh?*   VOH toots VAY

765. I have _____.   *Ich habe* _____.   isch HA-be

_____ a headache.   _____ *Kopfschmerzen.*
KOPF-shmair-tsen

_____ a sore throat.   _____ *Halsweh.*   HALTS-vay

_____ an ear ache.   _____ *Ohrenschmerzen.*
OH-ren-SHMAIR-tsen

_____ a migraine.   _____ *eine Migräne.*
EIN-e mee-GRAY-ne

766. Look, it's _____.   *Hier, es ist* _____.
Hee-ah, ess-ist

_____ infected.   _____ *entzündet.*   ent-TSEWN-det

_____ swollen.   _____ *geschwollen.*
ge-SHVAWL-en

767. I think I have the flu.   *Ich glaube, ich habe die Grippe.*
      isch GLAU-be isch HA-be dee GRIP-e

768. I have indigestion.   *Ich habe Verdauungstörungen.*
      isch HA-be fe-DOW-oongs-SHTEWR-oong-en

769. I have a rash.   *Ich habe einen Ausschlag.*
      isch HA-be EIN-en AUS-shlahg

770. I think I _____.   *Ich glaube, ich habe _____.*
      isch GLAU-be isch HA-be

      _____ broke my arm.   _____ *mir den Arm gebrochen.*
          MEER dain ARM ge-BRAWKH-en

      _____ broke my leg.   _____ *mir das Bein gebrochen.*
          MEER dass BINE ge-BRAWKH-en

      _____ sprained my ankle.
      _____ *mir den Knöchel verstaucht.*
          MEER dain KNEW-khel fer-SHTAUSCHT

      _____ hurt myself.   _____ *mich verletzt.*
          MISCH fe-LETST

771. My child is sick.   *Mein Kind ist krank.*
      mine KINT ist KRAHNK

772. I need a doctor.   *Ich brauche einen Arzt/eine Ärztin.*
      isch BRAU-khe EIN-en ARTST/EIN-e AYRTS-tin

773. May I please speak to a nurse?
      Kann ich eine Krankenschwester sehen?
      KANN isch EIN-e KRAHNK-en-SHVESS-tah ZAY-en

774. Where is the aide?
      Wo ist der Krankenpfleger/die Krankenpflegerin?
      **VOH ist dair KRAHNK-en-PFLAY-ger/dee-KRAHNK-en-
      PFLAY-ger-in**

775. Please take me to _____.
      Bitte bringen Sie mich _____.
      BIT-e BRING-en ZEE misch

      _____ a hospital.   _____ *ins Krankenhaus.*
          ins KRAHNK-en-house

      _____ the emergency room.   _____ *zur Notaufnahme.*
          tsoor NOHT-auf-NAH-meh

_____ a pharmacy.   _____ *zu einer Apotheke.*
tsoo EIN-ah AH-poh-TAY-ke

_____ a 24-hour pharmacy.
_____ *zu einer Notapotheke.*
tsoo EIN-ah NOHT-AH-poh-TAY-ke

776. Do we need to take him to the hospital?
Sollen wir ihn ins Krankenhaus bringen?
ZOLL-en VEE-ah EEN ins KRAHNK-en-house BRING-en

777. I'm having intestinal problems.   *Ich habe Darmprobleme.*
isch HA-be DAHM-proh-BLAY-meh

778. I have high blood pressure.
Ich habe einen hohen Blutdruck.
isch HA-be EIN-en HOH-en BLOOT-drook

779. Will you need to draw blood?   *Müssen Sie Blut nehmen?*
MEWSS-en zee BLOOT NAY-men

780. I am taking this medication.   *Ich nehme diese Medikamente.*
isch NAY-meh DEE-ze me-dee-kah-MENN-teh

781. I am diabetic.   *Ich bin Diabetiker. (m.)*
ISCH bin DEE-ah-BE-tick-ah

Ich bin Diabetikerin. (f.)   **ISCH bin DEE-ah-BE-tick-ah-rin**

782. I am pregnant.   *Ich bin schwanger.*
ISCH bin SHVAHNG-ah

783. I am allergic to aspirin.   *Ich bin allergisch gegen Aspirin.*
ISCH bin all-ERG-isch GAY-gen AS-pe-reen

784. I'm on the pill.   *Ich nehme die (Antibaby-)Pille.*
isch NAY-meh dee (ANN-tee-BAY-bee) Pill-e

785. I need antibiotics.   *Ich brauche Antibiotika.*
isch BRAU-khe ANN-tee-bee-OW-tee-ka

786. Is it serious?   *Ist es etwas Ernstes?*
IST ess ET-vass ERNS-tes

787. How are you feeling?   *Wie fühlen Sie sich?*
vee FEWL-en ZEE sisch

788. I'm feeling better, thanks.   *Es geht mir besser, danke.*
     ess GAYT meeah BESS-ah DAHN-ke

789. I don't feel well.   *Ich fühle mich nicht gut.*
     isch FEWL-e misch NISCHT goot

790. I'm feeling dizzy.   *Mir ist schwindlig.*
     meer ist SHWIND-lisch

791. I feel like throwing up.
     Ich glaube, ich muss mich übergeben.
     isch GLAU-be isch MOUSSE misch EW-be-GAY-ben

792. The situation is getting worse.   *Es wird schlimmer.*
     es veert SHLIM-mah

793. I'm resting.   *Ich ruhe mich aus.*   isch ROO-e misch AUS

794. May I have a receipt for my health insurance?
     Kann ich eine Quittung für die Versicherung haben?
     KANN isch EIN-e KVITT-oong FEWR dee fe-SISCH-ah-roong
     HA-ben

SEEING A DENTIST

795. Can you recommend a good dentist?
     Können Sie einen guten Zahnarzt empfehlen?
     KOENN-en zee EIN-en GOOT-en TSAN-ahrtst emp-FAY-len
     Können Sie eine gute Zahnärztin empfehlen?
     KOENN-en zee EIN-e GOOT-e TSAHN-ayrtst-in emp-FAY-len

796. I have a toothache.   *Ich habe Zahnschmerzen.*
     isch HA-be TSAHN-shmerts-en

797. Do I have a cavity?   *Habe ich ein Loch?*
     HA-be isch ein LOKH

798. I think I have an abscess.
     Ich glaube, ich habe einen Abszess.
     isch GLAU-be isch HA-be EIN-en AP-TSESS

799. I think I lost a crown.
     Ich glaube, ich habe eine Krone verloren.
     isch GLAU-be isch HA-be EIN-e CROH-ne fe-LAW-ren

800. It hurts. *Es tut weh.* **ESS toot VAY**

801. Can you _____. *Können Sie _____.*
     KOENN-en zee meer

     _____ give me a filling? _____ *meinen Zahn füllen?*
     MINE-en TSAHN FEWL-en

     _____ give me a temporary filling?
     _____ *meinen Zahn vorläufig füllen?*
     MINE-en TSAHN FOR-LOY-fisch FEWL-en

     _____ give me something for the pain?
     _____ *mir etwas gegen Schmerzen geben?*
     meer ET-vass GAY-gen SHMERTS-en GAY-ben

802. Does it need to be pulled? *Müssen Sie den Zahn ziehen?*
     MOOS-en ZEE dain TSAHN TSEE-en

803. I need to have my dentures fixed.
     Ich muss meine Zahnprothese richten lassen.
     isch MOUSSE MINE-e TSAHN-proh-tay-zeh RISCH-ten
     LASS-en

804. He/she wears braces. *Er/sie hat Zahnspangen.*
     AIR/ZEE hat TSAHN-SHPANG-en

SEEING AN OPTOMETRIST

805. I need to replace my contact lenses.
     Ich muss meine Kontaktlinsen erneuern.
     isch MOUSSE MINE-e kon-TAKT-lins-en ehr-NOY-ern

Chapter 7
Communications

POST OFFICE

806. Where is the nearest post office? *Wo ist die nächste Post?*
VOH ist dee NAYKHS-te PAWST

807. Is there a mailbox nearby? *Gibt es hier einen Briefkasten?*
GIPT ess HEE-ah EIN-en BREEF-kas-ten

808. I need to mail _____. *Ich muss _____ schicken.*
isch MOUSSE _____ SHICK-en

_____ a letter. _____ *einen Brief _____.*
EIN-en BREEF

_____ a postcard. _____ *eine Postkarte _____.*
EIN-e PAWST-kar-te

_____ a money order.
_____ *eine Geldanweisung _____.*
EIN-e GELT-ahn-VIZE-oong

_____ a packagev. _____ *ein Paket _____.*
EIN PAH-ket

809. I'd like to buy some stamps.
Ich möchte Briefmarken kaufen.
isch MEWSH-te BREEF-mar-ken KAUF-en

810. I need to send a registered letter.
Ich muss einen eingeschriebenen Brief senden.
isch MOUSSE EIN-en EIN-ge-SHREE-ben-en BREEF ZEN-den

811.   What's the postage for the US?
        Wieviel kostet ein Brief in die USA?
        vee-FEEL KOST-et ein-BREEF in dee OO-ESS-AH

TELEPHONE

812.   Where can I make a phone call?   *Wo kann ich telefonieren?*
        VOH KANN isch te-le-foh-NEER-en

813.   How much does it cost to call the U.S.?
        Wieviel kostet der Anruf in die USA?
        vee-FEEL KOST-et dair AHN-roof in dee OO-ESS-AH

814.   I'd like to buy a phone card, please.
        Eine Telefonkarte, bitte.   EIN-e te-le-fohn-kar-te BIT-e

815.   Do you have a phonebook, please?
        Haben Sie ein Telefonbuch, bitte?
        HA-ben ZEE ein te-le-fohn-bookh, BIT-e

816.   I'd like to phone home.
        Ich möchte nach Hause telefonieren.
        isch MEWSH-te nakh HAU-ze te-le-foh-NEER-en

817.   I'd like to make a collect call.
        Ich möchte einen R-Ruf machen.
        isch MEWSH-te EIN-en ERR-ROOF MAKH-en

818.   What is the number here?
        Was ist Ihre Telefonnummer hier?
        VASS ist EER-e te-le-FOHN-noom-uh HEE-ah

819.   Do you have the number for the American consulate?
        Haben Sie die Nummer für das amerikanische Konsulat?
        HA-ben ZEE dee NOOM-uh FEWR dass ah-mair-i-KAHN-
        isch-e kon-soo-LAHT

820.   I'd like to buy a cell phone.   *Ich möchte ein Handy kaufen.*
        isch MEWSH-te ein HAN-dee kauf-en

821.   May I see your flip and slider cellphones?
        Kann ich Ihre Klapp- und Sliderhandys sehen?
        KANN isch EER-e KLAPP oont SLIDE-ah-HAN-dees ZAY-en

822. Do you have cell-phone accessories?
      Führen Sie Handyzubehör?
      FEWR-en zee HAN-dee-TSOO-be-HEWR

823. Is there a contract?   *Brauche ich einen Vertrag?*
      BRAU-khe isch EIN-en fe-TRAHK

824. My number is _____.   *Meine Nummer ist _____.*
      MINE-e NOOM-uh ist

825. I'd like to speak to _____.
      Ich möchte mit _____ sprechen.
      isch MEWSH-te mit _____ SPHREKH-en

826. Hello?   *Hallo?*   **HALL-oh**

827. Who is calling?   *Wer ist am Apparat?*
      VAIR ist am AH-pah-RAHT

828. It's Ann calling.   *Hier spricht Ann.*
      HEE-ah SPHRISCHT ANN

829. I'll put you through to him/her.   *Ich verbinde.*
      isch fe-BIN-de

830. One moment, please/ Please hold on.   *Einen Moment, bitte.*
      EIN-en moh-MENT BIT-e

831. Can you call back?

      Können Sie zurückrufen? (formal, singular or plural)
      KOENN-en zee tsoo-REWK-roof-en

      Könnt ihr zurückrufen? (informal, plural)
      KOENNT EER tsoo-REWK-roof-en

      Kannst du zurückrufen? (informal, singular)
      KANNST doo tsoo-REWK-roof-en

832. It's busy.   *Besetzt.*   **be-ZETST**

833. Would you like to leave a message?

      Möchtet ihr eine Nachricht hinterlassen? (informal, plural)
      MEWSH-tet EE-ah EIN-e NAKH-rischt HIN-tah-LASS-en

      Möchtest du eine Nachricht hinterlassen? (informal, singular)
      MEWSH-test doo EIN-e NAKH-rischt HIN-tah-LASS-en

834. I'll call back later.   *Ich rufe später zurück.*
isch ROOF-e SPHAY-tah tsoo-REWK

835. We were cut off.   *Wir sind unterbrochen worden.*
VEE-ah zint oont-e-BROHKH-en VOR-den

836. I can't get the call to go through.
Ich bekomme keine Verbindung.
ISCH be-KOMM-e KEIN-e fe-BIN-doong

INTERNET, ELECTRONICS, AND COMPUTERS

In order to operate electronic equipment via a charger in Germany, Austria, and Switzerland, you will need an adapter that can handle 220/240 V. You should acquire one prior to your trip. Electronics supply stores usually carry adapters suited for international travel.

837. Where is the next Internet café?
Gibt es ein Internet-Cafe in der Nähe?
GIPT ess EIN IN-tah-net KAFF-aye IN dair NAY-eh

838. Is there high-speed Internet?
Gibt es hier High-Speed Internetzugang?
GIPT ess HEE-ah HIGH-SPEED INT-er-net-TSOO-gahng

839. Do you charge for Internet access or is it free?
Ist der Internetzugang kostenlos oder kostenpflichtig?
IST dair INT-er-net-TSOO-gahng KOST-en-los OH-dah
KOST-en-pflisch-tisch

840. How do I connect to the Internet?
Wie bekomme ich einen Internetzugang?
VEE be-KOMM-e ISCH EIN-en INT-er-net-TSOO-gahng

841. Do you have a printer I can use?
Haben Sie einen Drucker für mich?
HA-ben zee EIN-en DROO-ka FEWR misch

842. Can you print this out?   *Können Sie das ausdrucken?*
KOENN-en ZEE dass AUS-drook-en

843. How does the wireless router work?
Wie funktioniert der drahtlose Router?
VEE foonk-tsyoh-NEERT dair DRAHT-lowz-e ROUT-ah

844. Where can I buy a SIM card?
Wo kann ich eine SIM-Karte kaufen?
VOH KANN isch EIN-e ZIM-KAR-te KAUF-en

845. Do you sell _____?   *Verkaufen Sie _____?*
fe-KAUF-en ZEE

_____ adaptors.   _____ *Adapter.*   **ah-DAP-ter**

_____ chargers.   _____ *Batterieladegeräte.*
BAT-eh-REE-LAH-de-ge-RAY-te

_____ jump drives.   _____ *Speicher-Sticks.*
SHPY-schah-SHTIX

_____ USB sticks?   _____ *USB-Speicher-Sticks?*
OO-ESS-BAY-SHPY-schah-SHTIX

846. Where is a computer-repair store/computer store?
Gibt es hier eine Computerreparaturwerkstatt/einen Computerladen?
GIPT ess HEE-ah EIN-e com-PYOO-tuh-re-pah-ra-TOOR-VAIRK-shtat/EIN-en-com-PYOO-ta-LAH-den

847. What is the number for the computer repair store?
Wie lautet die Nummer der Computerreparaturwerkstatt?
VEE LAU-tet dee NOOM-ah dair com-PYOO-tuh-re-pah-ra-TOOR-VAIRK-shtat

848. Can you fix _____?
Können Sie _____ reparieren?
KOENN-en ZEE _____ re-pah-REER-en

_____ my laptop.   _____ *meinen Laptop.*
MINE-en LAP-top

_____ cellphone.   _____ *mein Handy.*
mine HAN-dee

_____ computer?   _____ *meinen Computer.*
MINE-en com-PYOO-ta

- Most German-speakers pronounce "@" ("at") in part of an address as "at."
- German makes a distinction between a plain battery (Batterie) and a rechargeable battery (Akku). Most computer batteries are Akkus.
- SMS, or short message service, is a wireless phone text service popular in Germany that allows for the exchange of short text messages. The verb is "simsen" (to send a text message).

849. corrupt. *defekt.* **day-FEKT**

850. cut and paste. *ausschneiden und einfügen.*
AUS-shny-den oont EIN-FEW-gen

851. disk drive. *Diskettenlaufwerk.* **dis-KETT-en-LAUF-vairk**

852. drag and drop. *ziehen und ablegen.*
TSEE-en oont AP-LAY-gen

853. hard (disk) drive. *Festplattenlaufwerk.*
FEST-platt-en-LAUF-vairk

854. icon. *Ikon.* **EE-kon**

855. log in/out/off. *einloggen/ ausloggen/ abmelden.*
EIN-LOGG-en, AUS-LOGG-en, AP-MELD-en

856. memory (RAM). *Speicher.* **SHPY-sheh**

857. next. *nächste.* **nex-te**

858. previous. *zurück.* **tsoo-REWK**

859. to finish, to complete. *fertigstellen.* **FER-tik-shtell-en**

860. operating system.
Betriebssystem (Mac OS X, Windows XP, etc.).
be-TREEPS-zys-taym

861. page. *Seite.* **ZYE-te**

862. power (on/off) button. *An/Ausschalter.* **AN/AUS-schal-tah**

863. printer. *Drucker.* **DROO-kah**

864. rechargeable battery. *Akku.* **AHK-oo**

865. return/enter key. *Eingabetaste.* **EIN-gah-be-TASS-te**

866. scroll. *blättern.* **BLETT-ern**

867. search engine. *Suchmaschine.* **ZOOKH-mah-SHEE-ne**

868. settings. *Einstellungen.* **EIN-shtel-oong-en**

869. download. *herunterladen.* **hair-OON-tah-LAH-den**

870. trash. *Papierkorb.* pah-PEE-ah-korp

871. turn on. *einschalten.* EIN-shal-ten

872. upload. *hochladen.* HOHKH-lah-den

873. user I.D. *Nutzerkennzeichen.*
NOO-tse-KENN-tseye-schen

874. tutorial. *Anleitung.* AN-lye-toong

875. wired. *verkabelt.* fe-KAH-belt

876. wireless. *drahtlos.* DRAHT-lohs

Chapter 8
Proverbs, Idiomatic Expressions, Cognates, Interjections, Slang

If you want to pepper your speech with idioms, typical German proverbs, or some juicy slang expressions, take a look at the entries below and start practicing right away, because "Übung macht den Meister" (practice makes perfect)!

PROVERBS

877. Everything must come to an end (only a sausage has two).
Alles hat ein Ende, nur die Wurst hat zwei.
ALL-es hat ein EN-de NOOR dee VOORST hat TSVY

878. To make a mountain out of a molehill.
Aus einer Mücke einen Elefanten machen.
aus ein-ah MEWK-e ein-en e-le-FANT-en MAKH-en

879. Striking the iron while it is hot.
Das Eisen schmieden, solange es heiß ist.
dass EYE-zen SHMEE-den zoh-LANG-e ess HEISS ist

880. That's outside the box!
Das fällt aus dem Rahmen (des Üblichen)!
DASS fellt aus daym RAHM-en (dess EWB-lisch-en)

881. I've had it up to here. / I'm sick of it.
Das hängt mir zum Hals heraus.
dass HAENGT meer tsoom HALTS her-aus

882. To not see the forest for the trees.
Den Wald vor lauter Bäumen nicht sehen.
dain VALT fawr LAUT-ah BOY-men nischt ZAY-en

883. The devil is in the details.   *Der Teufel steckt im Detail.*
dair TOY-fl SHTEKT im day-TIE

884. Buying a pig in a poke.   *Die Katze im Sack kaufen.*
dee KATS-e im ZAHK kau-fen

885. Lies are like snowballs: the farther they roll, the bigger they get.
*Lügen sind wie Schneebälle: je weiter man sie fortwälzt, desto
größer werden sie.*
LEW-gen ZINT vee SHNAY-bell-e yay VYTE-e mann zee
FORT-veltst DESS-toh GREWSS-e VAIR-den zee

886. To go through thick and thin.
Durch Dick und Dünn gehen.
DOORSCH DICK oont DEWNN gay-en

887. Even a blind squirrel finds nuts once in a while.
Ein blindes Huhn findet auch mal ein Korn.
EIN BLIN-des HOON FIN-det AUKH mahl ein KORN

888. A single swallow does not make a summer.
Eine Schwalbe macht noch keinen Sommer.
EIN-e SHWAHL-be MAKHT nohkh KEI-nen ZOMM-e

889. Looking for a needle in a haystack.
Eine Stecknadel im Heuhaufen suchen.
EIN-e SHTECK-nah-dl im HOY-hau-fen ZOOKH-en

890. One doesn't look into the mouth of a gift horse.
Einem geschenkten Gaul schaut man nicht ins Maul.
EIN-em ge-SHENK-ten GOWL shout man NISCHT ins
MOWL

891. She always gets right to the point.
Sie fällt immer mit der Tür ins Haus.
ZEE fellt IM-ah mit dair TEWR ins HOWS

892. He's got a hangover.   *Er hat einen Kater.*
AIR hat EIN-en KAH-tah

893. He's as stubborn as a mule.   *Er ist stur wie ein Maulesel.*
AIR ist SHTOO-ah vee ein MOWL-aye-zl

894. His bark is worse than his bite.
Hunde, die bellen, beißen nicht.
HOON-de dee BELL-en BEI-sen NISCHT

895. I wasn't born yesterday.   *Ich bin nicht von gestern.*
ISCH bin NISCHT fawn GUESS-tern

896. I'm out of the picture.   *Ich bin weg vom Fenster.*
ISCH bin VEK fawm FENS-tah

897. I'm the last one outta here.
Ich fahre mit dem Lumpensammler.
ISCH FAH-re mit daym LOOM-pen-ZAMM-lah

898. Clothes make the man (and the woman, too!).
Kleider machen Leute.
KLEYE-dah MAKH-en LOY-te

899. Chin up!   *Kopf hoch!*   **KAWPF HOHKH**

900. Easier said than done.   *Leichter gesagt als getan.*
LEISCH-tah ge-ZAHGT ALSS ge-TAHN

901. A bird in the hand is worth two in the bush.
Lieber ein Spatz in der Hand als eine Taube auf dem Dach.
**LEE-bah ein SHPAHTS in dair HANT ALS EIN-e TOW-be
AUF daym DAKH**

902. A leopard can't change his spots.
Man kann nicht über den eigenen Schatten springen.
**MANN KANN NISCHT EW-bah dayn EYE-ge-nen SHAT-en
SHPRING-en**

903. The early bird catches the worm.
Morgenstund' hat Gold im Mund.
MOR-gen-SHTOONT hat GOLT im MOONT

904. Time is money.   *Zeit ist Geld.*   **TSITE ist GELT**

905. He's always interrupting me.   *Er fällt mir immer ins Wort.*
AIR FELLT meer IMM-ah ins VORT

906. She's playing the prima donna.
Sie spielt die beleidigte Leberwurst.
zee SHPEELT dee be-LEYE-disch-te LAY-beh-VOORST

907. Too many cooks spoil the broth.
Viele Köche verderben den Brei.
FEEL-e KEWSCH-e fe-DER-ben dain BREYE

908. To kill two birds with one stone.
Zwei Fliegen mit einer Klappe schlagen.
TSVEYE FLEE-gen mit EIN-ah KLAP-e SHLAH-gen

909. Where there's a will, there's a way.
Wo ein Wille ist, ist auch ein Weg.
VOH ein VIL-e ist ist aukh ein VAYK

910. To understand is to forgive.   *Verstehen ist Vergeben.*
fe-SHTAY-en ist fe-GAY-ben

911. Strike while the iron is hot.
Man muss das Eisen schmieden, solange es heiß ist.
mann MOUSSE dass EYE-zen SHMEE-den zoh-LANG-e es HEISS ist

912. Better late than never.   *Besser spät als nie.*
BESS-ah SHPAYT als NEE

913. Clothes make the man.   *Kleider machen Leute.*
KLIDE-ah MAHKH-en LOY-te

914. Rome wasn't built in a day.
Rom ist auch nicht an einem Tag erbaut worden.
ROWM ist oukh NISHT un INE-am TAWK er-bout VAWR-dan

915. All's well that ends well.   *Ende gut, alles gut.*
EN-deh GOOT AL-es GOOT

916. Practice makes perfect.   *Übung macht den Meister.*
EW-boong mahkht dayn MEYE-stah

917. Every cloud has a silver lining.
Jedes Unglück hat auch sein Gutes.
YAY-des OON-glewk HAT aukh zine GOOT-es

918. No sooner said than done.   *Gesagt, getan.*
ge-ZAHGT ge-TAHN

919. Beggars can't be choosers.
In der Not frisst der Teufel Fliegen.
IN dair NOHT frisst dair TOY-fl FLEE-gen

920. Try before you trust.   *Trau, schau, wem.*
TRAU SHAU VAYM

921. He's an old hand.   *Er ist ein alter Hase.*
AIR ist- ein AL-tah HAHZ-e

922. When it rains, it pours.   *Ein Unglück kommt selten allein.*
EIN OON-glewk kommt ZEL-ten ahl-EIN

IDIOMATIC EXPRESSIONS

923. She's in seventh heaven.   *Sie ist im siebten Himmel.*
ZEE ist im SEEB-ten HIM-l

924. He's pouting.   *Er schmollt.*   air SHMOLLT

925. She's crazy!   *Sie spinnt!*   zee SHPINNT

926. She's got a loose screw!   *Sie hat eine Schraube locker.*
zee HAT EIN-e SHRAU-be LOK-ah

927. That man/woman is definitely insane!
Der Mann/dieFrau ist total bekloppt!
dair MANN/dee-FRAU ist toh-TAHL be-KLOPPT

928. I'm depressed.   *Ich bin niedergeschlagen.*
ISCH bin NEE-dah-ge-SHLAH-gen

929. I'm fed up!   *Mir reichts!*   MEER REISCHTS

930. He seems completely dazed.   *Er ist völlig daneben.*
AIR ist FEWLL-isch da-NAY-ben

931. She's such a fraidy cat!   *Sie ist so ein Angsthase!*
zee ist ZOH ein ANGST-hahz-e

932. I'm exhausted!   *Ich bin fix und fertig!*
ISCH bin FIX oont FER-tisch

933. He's lost his marbles.   *Er hat sie nicht mehr alle.*
air HAT ZEE nischt mair ALL-e

934. I am so lazy!   *Ich bin ein Faulpelz!*
ISCH bin ein FAUL-pelts

935. We are so lucky!   *Wir haben Schwein gehabt!*
VEER HA-ben SHVINE ge-HAPT

936.   He stood me up.   *Er hat mich versetzt.*
       AIR hat misch fe-SETST

937.   She is so fickle.   *Sie ist so flatterhaft.*
       ZEE ist zoh FLATT-ah-haft

938.   He's a real ladies' man.   *Er ist ein Frauenheld.*
       AIR ist ein FRAU-en-helt

939.   He's sweet talking me.   *Er raspelt Süßholz.*
       air RAHSP-elt SEWSS-holts

940.   I have a crush on her.   *Ich steh' auf sie.*
       isch SHTAY auf ZEE

941.   S/he is hopelessly in love with me!
       Er/sie ist total verknallt in mich!
       air/zee ist toh-TAHL fe-KNALLT in misch

942.   It was love at first sight.   *Es war Liebe auf den ersten Blick.*
       ESS vahr LEE-be auf dain AIRS-ten BLIK

943.   She's pretty enough to eat!   *Sie ist zum Anbeissen!*
       zee ist tsoom AN-byss-en

944.   She is simply stunning!   *Sie ist einfach umwerfend!*
       zee ist EIN-fakh OOM-verf-ent

945.   She has a crush on him.   *Sie schwärmt für ihn.*
       zee SHWAERMT fewr EEN

946.   He's going to dump me.   *Er gibt mir bald den Laufpass.*
       air GIPT meer BALT dain LAUF-pass

COGNATES

Cognates are words in two languages that share a similar meaning, spelling, and pronunciation. Since German and English share a great deal of linguistic history, there is an abundance of cognates. Cognates are useful to know when traveling in a German-speaking country. The list below gives the hundred most-common cognates—they look like the English word, and they have almost exactly the same meaning.

Aktiv, alle, der Arm, backen, beginnen, bevor, binden, bitter, blind, blond, brauen, bringen, der Bulle, der Bus, die Butter, direkt, der Doktor/die Doktorin, das Drama, die Droge, der Dung, das Eis, elektrisch, Ende, fein, fett, die Flamme; die Form, das Gold, Golf, das Gramm, das Gras, gratulieren, die Gruppe, der Hammer, die Hand, hängen, hier, hindern, das Hotel, der Humor, ideal, intelligent, das Kabel, die Kamera, das Kilo, der Knoten, kompliziert, kosten, der Kredit, die Kritik, die Kultur, die Lampe, lernen, die Lippe, die Liste, der Liter, die Maschine, die Maus, die Medizin, das Metall, der Meter, mild, die Million, modern, der Moment, die Musik, der Name, nervös, packen, das Papier, die Pause, der Plan, die Polizei, die Qualität, der Rest, das Resultat, das Rezept, der Sand, der Schuh, das Schwein, die Sekunde, singen, sinken, die Sorte, der Sport, stinken, die Summe, die Temperatur, das Tempo, der Text, der Titel, die Tradition, trinken, die Universität, warm, wenn, wild, der Wind, der Winter, der Zoo.

INTERJECTIONS

947.   Great!   *Prima!*   **PREE-mah**

948.   Super!   *Toll!*   **TAWLL**

949.   That's hot!   *Das ist echt geil!*   **dass ist ESCHT GYLE**

950.   Whatever!   *Wie auch immer!*   **VEE aukh IM-eh**

951.   I dare you!   *Trau dich doch!*   **TRAU DISCH dokh**

952.   Who cares?   *Das ist mir egal!*   **DASS ist meer aye-GAHL**

953.   I don't care!   *Na und!*   **na OONT**

954.   Darn!   *So ein Mist!*   **SOH EIN MIST**

955.   Oh rats!   *Ach Mann!*   **AKH MANN**

956.   Whoopsie-daisy!   *Hoppla!*   **HAWP-lah**

957.   Damn!   *Verdammt*   **fe DAHMT**

958.   Shit.   *Scheiße!*   **SHY seh**

959.   Yum yum!   *O, wie lecker!*   **OH vee LECK-ah**

960. How stupid!   *Echt blöd!*   **ESCHT BLEWT**

961. What a dump!   *Was für ein Schuppen!*
      VASS fewr ein SHOOP-en

962. Yuck!   *Grausig!*   **GROUS-isch**

963. Ew!   *Eklig!*   **EHK-lik**

964. That's a bunch of bull!   *Das ist ganz großer Mist!*
      DASS ist GANTS GROHS-sah MIST

965. Really cute!   *Echt süß!*   **ESCHT ZEWS**

966. What a mess!   *Was für eine Bescherung!*
      VASS fewr ein-e be-SHARE-oong

967. Mind your own business!   *Geht dich nichts an!*
      GAYT disch NISCHTS an

968. Get out!   *Raus!*   **ROUS**

969. That's the bomb!   *Das ist echt der Hammer!*
      DASS ist ECHT dair HAMM-ah

970. Dear me!   *Ach du liebe Zeit!*   **AKH doo LEE-be TSITE**

SLANG

The following slang expressions are commonly used in informal conversation. The standard English equivalent of the English slang word appears at the end of the first sentence, where appropriate.

971. We just bought a jalopy. (a car)
      Wir haben uns gerade 'ne alte Karre gekauft.
      VEE-ah HA-ben oons ge-RAH-de ne AL-te KAR-e ge-KAUFT

972. I make a hundred big ones a day. (Euros/dollars)
      Ich mache pro Tag hundert Mäuse.
      isch MAH-khe PRO TAHK HOON-dert MOY-ze

973. I hate the grub here. (food)   *Ich hasse den Fraß hier.*
      isch HASS-e dain FRAHSS hee-ah

974. We really chowed down. (ate)   *Wir haben echt reingehauen.*
      VEE-ah HA-ben ECHT RINE-ge-HOW-en

975. She just got a job!   *Sie hat einen Job gelandet!*
      ZEE hat EIN-en SHOB ge-LAN-det

976. Can you lend me this trashy book?
      Kannst du mir den Schmöker leihen?
      KANNST doo mee-ah dain SHMEW-kah LIE-en

977. Let's beat it! (leave)   *Hauen wir ab!*   **HOW-en VEE-ah AP**

978. She is chatting with her best friend.
      Sie plaudert mit ihrer besten Freundin.
      zee PLOW-det mit EER-ah BEST-en FROYN-din

979. How about watching a schmaltzy flick tonight? (movie)
      Sollen wir uns heute Abend eine Schnulze ansehen?
      ZAWL-en VEE-ah oons HOY-te AH-bent EIN-e SCHNOOL-tseh AN-zay-en

980. I love your new clothes.
      Ich finde deine neuen Klamotten toll.
      isch FIN-de DYE-ne NOY-en KLAH-mott-en TOLL

981. That's a crazy idea!   *Das ist echt bekloppt!*
      DASS ist ECHT be-KLOPPT

982. That is really crazy.
      Da wird doch der Hund in der Pfanne verrückt.
      da VEERT dokh dair HOONT in dair PFAN-e fe-REWKT

983. I love your new crib. (place)   *Ich finde deine neue Hütte toll.*
      isch FIN-de DYE-ne NOY-e HEWT-e TAWL

984. That lout is getting on my nerves. (man)
      Der Typ geht mir auf die Nerven.
      dair TEWP gayt meer auf dee NER-fen

985. I know that jerk.   *Ich kenn' den Knilch.*
      isch KENN dayn KNILSCH

986. What an ugly rag! (dress)   *Was für ein Fetzen!*
      VASS fewr ein FETS-en

987.   That is a really loony story.   *Das ist eine echt doofe Story.*
        DASS ist EIN-e EKHT DOH-fe SHTAW-ree

988.   I don't understand a thing!   *Ich versteh' Bahnhof!*
        isch fe-SHTAY BAHN-hohf

989.   He is two donuts short of a dozen. (unintelligent)
        Er ist dumm wie Bohnenstroh.
        AIR ist DOOM vee BOH-nen-SHTROH

990.   What a stupid! (blockhead)   *Was für ein blöder Dummkopf!*
        VASS fewr INE BLEW-dah doohm-kopf

991.   Give me that whatchamacallit!   *Gib mir das Dingsda!*
        GIP meer dass DINGS-da

992.   It's all a load of nonsense!   *Das ist doch alles Unfug!*
        DASS ist dokh ALL-es OON-fook

993.   He's acting the fool.   *Er macht auf blöd.*
        air MAKHT auf BLEWD

994.   I don't see the fun of it.   *Ich finde das gar nicht lustig.*
        isch FIN-de dass GAHR nischt LOOSS-tisch

995.   Piece of cake! (easy)   *Kinderspiel!*   **KIN-dah-SHPEEL**

996.   I can't believe it!   *Ich fass' es nicht!*
        isch FASS ess NISCHT

997.   Pigs will fly first! (it is very unlikely to happen)
        Da müsste schon ein Wunder geschehen
        dah MEWS-te SHOHN ein VOON-dah ge-SHAY-en

998.   That's a sure thing!   *Klarer Fall!*   **KLAH-rah FAHLL**

999.   I'll be damned if I know!   *Ich habe keinen blassen Dunst!*
        isch HAH-be KEIN-en BLAHSS-en DOONST

1000.   You don't say!   *Was Sie nicht sagen!*
        VASS ZEE nischt ZAH-gen

1001.   I have other irons in the fire. (I have options.)
        Ich hab' noch andere Eisen im Feuer.
        isch HAHB nokh AN-de-re EYE-zen im FOY-ah

Appendix
Language Structures and Parts of Speech

Nouns

Articles and Gender

As in English, German has two categories of article, definite and indefinite. The English definite article "the" corresponds to the German articles "der," "die," "das" (singular) and "die" (plural) in the nominative case. When you learn a new word, try to learn the gender-identifying article with it.

Der Mann	die Frau	das Kind	die Männer, die Frauen, die Kinder
The man	the woman	the child	the men, the women, the children
Masc. Sing.	**Fem. Sing.**	**Neut. Sing.**	**Masc., Fem., Neut. Plural**

The English indefinite articles "a" and "an" correspond to the German articles "ein" (m. and n.) and "eine" (f.). Look at the examples below.

Ein Mann	Eine Frau	Ein Kind
A man	A woman	A child
Masc. Sing.	**Fem. Sing.**	**Neut. Sing.**

Gender, Case, and Number

German has four cases: nominative, genitive, dative, and accusative. In the chart below, note how articles and nouns change according to case:

Case	Function of noun	Examples			
		Masculine	Feminine	Neuter	Plural
Nominative	Subject—who? What?	**Der Mann** ist nett. The man is nice.	**Die Frau** ist jung. The woman is young.	**Das Kind** ist klein. The child is little.	**Die Männer** sind nett. **Die Frauen** sind jung. **Die Kinder** sind klein. The men are nice. The women are young. The children are little.
Genitive	Possession—whose?	Das Auto **des Mannes.** The man's car	die Tasche **der Frau.** The woman's pocketbook	die Banane **des Kindes.** the child's banana.	die Autos **der Männer,** die Taschen **der Frauen,** die Bananen **der Kinder.** The mens' cars. The women's pocketbooks. The children's bananas.
Dative	Indirect Object—to whom?	Ich gebe **dem Mann** Geld. I give money to the man.	Ich gebe **der Frau** Geld. I give money to the woman.	Ich gebe **dem Kind** eine Banane. I give a banana to the child.	Ich gebe **den Männern** Geld. Ich gebe **den Frauen** Geld. Ich gebe **den Kindern** Bananen. I give money to the men. I give money to the women. I give bananas to the children.
Accusative	Direct Object—whom? what?	Ich sehe **den Mann.** I see the man.	Ich sehe **die Frau.** I see the woman.	Ich sehe **das Kind.** I see the child.	Ich sehe **die Männer.** Ich sehe **die Frauen.** Ich sehe **die Kinder.** I see the men. I see the women. I see the children.

Adjectives

As in English, adjectives in the **final position** of a German sentence do not change from their original form and are not influenced by the gender, case, or number of any of the nouns in the sentence. Take a look at these examples:

Der Mann ist **nett**.	Ich finde den Mann **nett**.
The man is nice.	I find the man to be nice.
Die Frau ist **nett**.	Ich finde die Frau **nett**.
The woman is nice.	I find the woman to be nice.
Das Kind ist **klein**.	Ich finde das Kind **klein**.
The child is small.	I find the child to be small.
Die Studenten sind **nett**.	Ich finde die Studenten **nett**.
The students are nice.	I find the students to be **nice**.

As in English, German adjectives are placed **directly before the nouns** they modify:

Ich möchte ein **interessantes Buch** finden.
I want to find an interesting book.

Wir haben ein **tolles Hotel** gefunden.
We found a great hotel.

Unlike English, German adjectives preceding, and thus modifying, a noun must agree with its gender, case, and number. Also, a slight adjustment to the appearance of the adjective may sometimes be necessary to achieve this agreement.

Depending on the case and number of the noun, the definite articles used can be "der," "die," "das," "den," "dem,"or "des." When the adjective preceding the noun is combined with a definite article, the adjective ending is either –e or –en. Take a look at the chart below.

Definite article with adjective and noun (singular and plural):

Case	Function of noun	Examples			
		Masculine	Feminine	Neuter	Plural
Nominative	Subject—who? What?	Der nette Mann trinkt Kaffee. The nice man drinks coffee.	Die nette Frau trinkt Kaffee. The nice woman drinks coffee.	Das nette Kind trinkt Milch. The nice child drinks milk.	Die netten Männer trinken Kaffee. Die netten Frauen trinken Kaffee. Die netten Kinder trinken Milch. The nice men drink coffee. The nice women drink coffee. The nice children drink milk.
Genitive	Possession—whose?	Das Auto des alten Mannes. The old man's car	die Tasche der alten Frau. The old woman's car	die Banane des kleinen Kindes. The little child's banana	die Kinder der alten Männer; die Kinder der alten Frauen; die Schnuller der kleinen Kinder. The old men's children. The old women's children. The little children's pacifiers
Dative	Indirect Object—to whom?	Ich gebe dem alten Mann Geld. I give money to the old man.	Ich gebe der alten Frau Geld. I give money to the old woman.	Ich gebe dem kleinen Kind eine Banane. I give a banana to the little child.	Ich gebe den alten Männern Geld; ich gebe den alten Frauen Geld; ich gebe den kleinen Kindern Bananen. I give money to the old men. I give money to the old women. I give bananas to the little children.
Accusative	Direct Object—whom? What?	Ich sehe den alten Mann. I see the old man.	Ich sehe die alte Frau. I see the old woman.	Ich sehe das kleine Kind. I see the little child.	Ich sehe die alten Männer. Ich sehe die alten Frauen. Ich sehe die kleinen Kinder. I see the old men. I see the old women. I see the little children.

Depending on the case and number of the noun, the indefinite articles used can be "ein," "eine," "einem," "eines," "einer," or "einen." When the adjective is paired with an indefinite article, then the adjective ending is either –e, –es, –er, or –en. Take a look at the chart below.

Indefinite article with adjective and noun (only singular):

Case	Function of noun	Examples		
		Masculine	Feminine	Neuter
Nominative	Subject—who? What?	**Ein** net-ter Mann trinkt Kaffee. A nice man is drinking coffee.	**Eine** nette Frau trinkt Kaffee. A nice woman is drinking coffee.	**Ein** nettes Kind trinkt Milch. A nice child is drinking milk.
Genitive	Possession—whose?	Das Auto **eines** alten Mannes. The old man's car.	die Tasche **einer** alten Frau. The old woman's car.	die Banane **eines** kleinen Kindes. The little child's banana.
Dative	Indirect Object—to whom?	Ich gebe **einem** alten Mann Geld. I give money to an old man.	Ich gebe **einer** alten Frau Geld. I give money to an old woman.	Ich gebe **einem** kleinen Kind eine Banane. I give a banana to a little child.
Accusative	Direct Object—whom? What?	Ich sehe **einen** alten Mann. I see an old man.	Ich sehe **eine** alte Frau. I see an old woman.	Ich sehe **ein** kleines Kind. I see a little child.

Adverbs

As in English, adverbs in German follow the verb they modify, but, unlike English, there is no difference in form between a German adjective and its corresponding adverb.

Adjective	Adverb
Die Frau ist **langsam**.	Die Frau arbeitet **langsam**.
The woman is **slow**.	The woman works **slowly**.

Subject pronouns

Ich (I)	Wir (We)
Du (You—informal)	Ihr (You—plural, informal)
Er, Sie, Es (He, She, It)	Sie (They—plural and You formal, singular and plural)

Sometimes you might hear German speakers using "man" (one) rather than "wir" for "we."

Verbs

Conjugation

The following present-tense conjugations are useful, as all three verbs are used frequently in everyday conversation.

Haben: to have

Ich habe (I have)	Wir haben (we have)
Du hast (you have, informal)	Ihr habt (you have, informal, plural)
Er/sie/es/hat (he, she, it has)	Sie haben (they have, You have, formal, singular and plural)

Sein: to be

Ich bin (I am)	Wir sind (we have)
Du bist (you are, informal)	Ihr seid (you have, informal, plural)
Er/sie/es ist (he, she, it is)	Sie sind (they have, You have, formal, singular and plural)

Machen: to do

Ich mache (I do)	Wir machen (we do)
Du machst (you do, informal)	Ihr macht (you do, informal, plural)
Er/sie/es macht (he, she, it does)	Sie machen (they do, You do, formal, singular and plural)

Commands (Imperatives)

In German, there are three different verb forms for the imperative or command form, corresponding to the three different forms of "you": the informal "du" (singular) and "ihr" (plural), and the formal "Sie" (singular and plural).

Example: to come—**kommen**

Informal, addressing one person	**Komm!**	Come!
Informal, when addressing groups	**Kommt!**	Come!
Formal, one or more people	**Kommen Sie!**	Come!

Example: to sleep—**schlafen**

Informal, addressing one person	**Schlaf jetzt!**	Sleep now!
Informal, when addressing groups	**Schlaft jetzt!**	Sleep now!
Formal, one or more people	**Schlafen Sie jetzt!**	Sleep now!

Example: to eat—**essen**

Informal, addressing one person	**Iss!**	Eat!
Informal, when addressing groups	**Esst!**	Eat!
Formal, one or more people	**Essen Sie!**	Eat!

Word Order

Just as in English, the word order in German follows the pattern S (subject)—V (verb)—O (object).

Ich	sehe	das Hotel.
I	see	the hotel. (English)
S	V	O

Negation

In order to make a sentence negative, place the word "nicht" after the part you wish to negate.

Ich	sehe	das Hotel **nicht.**
I don't	see	the hotel.

Since in the above sentence you wish to stress the fact that it is the **hotel** you do not see, place the "nicht" right after "das Hotel."

Extended Word Order

If you want to add time, manner, and place to a sentence, maintain the following order:

Wir	**fahren**	um sieben Uhr	mit dem Zug	nach Hamburg.
S	V	**time**	**manner**	**place**
(Position 1)	(Position 2)			
We	travel	to Hamburg	by train	at seven o'clock.
S	V	**place**	**manner**	**time**

In German, the core of a sentence is the conjugated verb, which is always in second position. Thus, when you add components such as time, manner, or place to the beginning of a sentence—which is also known as position 1—you need to reverse the subject and the verb in order to maintain the verb's position.

Um sieben Uhr	<u>fahren</u>	wir mit dem Zug nach Hamburg.
(Position 1)	(Position 2)	
At seven o'clock	we travel to Hamburg by train.	

If you have two or more verbs in a sentence, the conjugated verb stays in second position, while all other verbs are in the final position (unconjugated) at the end of the sentence.

Ich	**möchte**	ein Eis **essen.**
	(Conjugated Verb, pos. 2)	(second verb in base form, final position)
I	**want to**	eat ice cream.

Ich	**möchte** nicht	mit dir essen gehen.
	(Conjugated Verb, pos. 2)	(second and third verbs in base form, final position)
I	don't want to	eat with you.

Dependent Clauses

In a dependent clause, the conjugated verb always goes at the end of the clause. A dependent clause is always separated by a comma from the main clause.

Ich weiß nicht,	warum du böse auf mich **bist**.
(independent clause: conjugated verb in 2nd pos.)	(dependent clause: conjugated verb in final position)
I don't know	why you **are** mad at me.
(main clause)	(dependent clause)

Now switch gears and whet your appetite for your upcoming trip by checking out the resources that follow.

More Learning Resources

[current at time of publication]

Goethe Institute—the pre-eminent resource on everything German
http://www.goethe.de/enindex.htm

German News, Info, Online Language Learning, German Radio
http://www.dw-world.de/

German Language, Culture, Books, Lessons, Vocabulary, DVDs,
Blogs, Chat, and more!
http://www.aboutgerman.net/index.htm

Official web site for travel planning of the German National Tourist
Office
http://www.cometogermany.com

Open Source Travel Guide
http://wikitravel.org/en/Germany

Germany Flights and Travel Guide
http://www.cheapflights.com/flight-guide-to-germany/

Travel information including Background Notes, entry and exit
requirements, safety and security, crime, health and transport.
http://travel.state.gov/travel/cis_pa_tw/cis/cis_1123.html

Germany Travel Advice
http://www.fco.gov.uk/en/travel-and-living-abroad/travel-advice
-by-country/europe/germany

Travels Through Germany
http://www.travelsthroughgermany.com/

Germany Vacations, Tourism, and Travel Reviews
http://www.tripadvisor.com/Tourism-g187275-Germany-Vacations
  .html

Online dictionary
http://Dict.leo.org

Index

A

abscess, 98
address, 7, 17
Adjectives, 119
Adverbs, 121
airline, 34
airport, 34, 40
allergic, 48, 97
allergies, 92
allergy, 48
American, 5, 20, 21
antibiotics, 97
APPENDIX: LANGUAGE
    STRUCTURES AND PARTS
    OF SPEECH, 117
appetizer, 51, 55–56
Appetizers, Lunch Items and Salad,
    55–56
Articles and Gender, 117
ATM, 19, 73
ATM card, 19, 73
attractions, 68

B

baggage, 35, 36
bank, 12, 73
Banking and Money, 73
Beverages, 62–64
bill, 52
boarding pass, 35
bookstore, 75, 80
breakfast, 45–47, 53
Breakfast Food, 53–54
bus, 19, 30, 38, 39
bus station, 19, 30, 38, 39

C

camera, 76, 86, 87
camping, 72
car, 32, 33, 44
cash, 73, 74
cell phone, 67, 101, 102
check-in, 35

children, 2, 68, 76, 80, 92
church, 65, 69
clothing, 75–77
Cognates, 112
coins, 85
collect call, 101
Colors, 89
Commands (Imperatives), 123
comprehensive insurance, 33
computer, 103–106
computer repair store, 104
Conjugation, 122
consulate, 20, 101
credit card, 19, 74
currency, 73
customs, 36
Customs and Baggage, 36

D

declare, 36
dentist, 98
departure, 35
Dependent clauses, 125
Dessert, 47, 48, 51, 60
Difficulties and Repairs, 17–19
Dining out, 49–51
dinner, 5, 46, 47
discount, 30, 31
doctor, 3, 92, 95–97
drive, 32, 33
driver's license, 32, 33
drugstore, 93–94

E

e-mail address, 67
emergency room, 96
e-ticket, 32
Extended Word Order, 124
eyes, 15

F

food, *see* Dining, Mealtimes
Friends and Social Networking, 66
Fruits and Vegetables, 58–59

G

gas, 33
gas station, 33
Gender, xii
Gender, Case, and Number, 117, 119
glasses, 20, 79
Greetings, Introductions,
    and Social Conversation,
    1–7
guided walk, 43

H

hair salon, 76, 87
health food, 75
health insurance, 98
help, 11, 12, 18, 19, 29
high-speed Internet connection,
    103
hiking, 43, 72, 80
hospital, 96, 97
hotel, 12, 17, 44, 45
hours, 68
Houses of Worship, 65

I

Idiomatic Expressions, 000
Interjections, 113
Internet, Electronics, and
    Computers, 103–106
itinerary, 32

K

key, 18, 45, 105

L

laptop, 104
laundromat, 85
laundry service, 85
Leisure Activities and Hobbies,
    70–71

local bus, 30, 38
log in/out/off, 105
lost-and-found desk, 20
luggage, 35
lunch, 46, 47, 55–56

M

mail, 100
mailbox, 100
main course, 51
Main Course, 57
Making Yourself Understood, 8–9
Measurements, 88
meat, 48, 56, 83
medication, 20, 91–93, 97
memory card, 86
menu, 50, 51
Menu: General items, 52
money, 19, 73
money order, 100
More Learning Resources,
    127–128
mosque, 65
movie, 69, 70
museum, 69
music, 71

N

name, 1, 44
Negation, 124
newsstand, 76, 87
Nouns, xii, 117, 119
Numbers and Telling Time, 20, 22
nurse, 96

O

opera, 69
operating system, 105

P

pain, 92, 99
passport, 18, 30, 36

passport check, 36
pharmacy, 91, 92, 97
phone, 7, 67, 101–104
phone card, 101
photography, 71
plane, 19
police station, 20
Post Office, 100
postage, 101
prescription, 91, 92, 93
price, 33, 68
printer, 103, 105

R

refundable, 31
religion, 71
rental agency (car), 32
repairs, 17–20, 81, 104
reservation, 29, 32, 34, 44
restaurant, 12, 49, 50
restroom, 12
return/enter key, 105
room, 44, 45

S

salad, 48, 55, 56, 59, 60
seafood, 49, 57
Seeing a Dentist, 98
Seeing a Doctor, 95–97
shoes, 43, 80
shopping, 73–87
sick, 95, 96
Sightseeing, 67–69
SIM card, 104
size, 79
Slang, 114–116
sports, 71, 72
stamps, 82, 100
stationer's, 75
stop-over, 36
store, 75–81, 86
Subject pronouns, 122
subway, 41
sunscreen, 79, 94
supermarket, 75, 83, 91
synagogue, 65

T

TV, 45
Taking the Bus, 38
Taking the Subway, 41
Talking about Mealtimes and
    Eating: General Expressions,
    46–48
Talking about the Weather and Seasons,
    25–27
Talking about Times of Day, Days of
    the Week, and Months, 23
taxi stand, 39
Telephone, 101–102
Tickets, 30, 31, 38, 39, 68
time, 20–23
tip, 52
train, 19, 23, 30, 36–38, 41
train station, vii, 12, 36, 40
travel agency, 29
Travel: General Vocabulary and
    Expressions, 28–29
traveler's checks, 19, 73
Traveling by car, 32–33
Traveling on Foot, 42–43
Traveling on Two Wheels, 42–43

U

USB cable, 86
USB sticks, 104
user I.D., 106

V

vacancy, 44
vegetarian, 48, 50, 58
Verbs, 122–124
visa, 30

W

weather, 25–27
web site, 7
window shopping, 74
Word Order, 123–124